Husna's
Story

Husna's Story

My wife, the Christchurch
massacre & my journey
to forgiveness

Farid Ahmed

with Kimberley Davis

ALLEN&UNWIN
SYDNEY·MELBOURNE·AUCKLAND·LONDON

Contents

Forewords

    Hon Lianne Dalziel, Mayor of Christchurch   7

    Te Maire Tau (Upoko, Ngāi Tūāhuriri),
    Associate Professor, University of Canterbury   9

    Professor Mohamad Abdalla, Director of the
    Centre for Islamic Thought and Education,
    University of South Australia   10

    Professor Mark Compton AM GCStJ,
    Lord Prior of the Order of St John   12

Preface   15

I   Days like any other   23

1.   One Monday   25
2.   One Friday   37

II   Husna   49

3.   Wisdom   51
4.   Trust   60
5.   Courage   69
6.   Determination   77
7.   Success   89
8.   Acceptance   97

9.	Generosity	104
10.	Empathy	112
11.	Kindness	117
12.	Love	122

III	The worst of acts	133
13.	Before	135
14.	During	139
15.	After	149
16.	Outside	161

IV	To God we belong	175
17.	Going home	177
18.	Telling Shifa	187
19.	Moving forward	199
20.	Waiting, waiting	213
21.	The following Friday	222

V	Love, above all	237
22.	A true hero	239
23.	Forgiveness	247
24.	Choose love	267
25.	Our shared duty	278

| Tributes to Husna | 283 |
| About the author | 319 |

Forewords

Hon Lianne Dalziel, Mayor of Christchurch

We all came to know Farid Ahmed in the aftermath of the tragic events of 15 March 2019. We knew him as a grieving husband whose wife, Husna Ahmed, was one of the 51 people who were killed that day. This is *Husna's Story*.

We knew Farid because of his moving address at the National Remembrance Service where, despite his grief, he spoke of peace and love and expressed an infinite capacity for forgiveness.

His words touched our hearts:

> *A volcano has anger, fury, rage. It doesn't have peace. It has hatred, it burns itself within, and it burns its surroundings. I don't want to have a heart like this, and I believe no one does. I want a heart that is full of love and care, and full of mercy, and will forgive lavishly, because this heart doesn't want any more life to be lost.*

This heart doesn't like that any human being should go through the pain I have gone through. That's why I have chosen peace, love, and I have forgiven.

And the message that resonated across the world was: This is how we respond to terrorism—not with hate and retribution, but with generosity of mind and spirit. This is how we build bridges across cities and across the world.

In his Easter message, Prince Charles referred to this 'remarkable example of forgiveness following the utterly appalling attack on Muslims in Christchurch, New Zealand' and described Farid as 'a shining example to us all'. I am so glad that Prince Charles and Farid were able to meet each other in person here in Christchurch.

And I am glad that through Farid's words we can all meet Husna. This book brings her story to life. We see her; we see the kindness, bravery, generosity and wisdom that defined her life and influenced all those around her.

In her own way, Husna has enabled forgiveness to come to the fore. We learn in this book how her own lived experience of love and forgiveness made her a role model in more ways than one.

We also know that Husna died a hero, living up to the values that guided her whole life, right to the very end. These values live on in *Husna's Story*; they are values we can all give meaning to by being kind, generous and courageous in every aspect of our lives.

Farid tells us that by sharing *Husna's Story* we can, as he has, become ambassadors for peace, love and forgiveness. We owe it to the memory of all those who died to do so.

Te Maire Tau (Upoko, Ngāi Tūāhuriri),
Associate Professor, University of Canterbury

Farid Ahmed is one of the survivors of the dreadful terrorist attack perpetrated against the Ōtautahi/Christchurch Muslim community on 15 March 2019. Tragically, his beloved wife, Husna, was one of the victims whose lives were taken.

Many of us may think that if a tragedy of this magnitude were to befall us our story would end there; the loss tearing a wound in our hearts that we could not move past. Farid's story provides ample testimony to the grief and suffering that he and his community have endured—but this tragedy is very far from the culmination of his story. In fact, he ardently refuses to terminate matters there.

Instead, what arises from these pages is an incredibly moving dedication to Husna, a memoir of his unflagging love for her, as well as a celebration of her love and generosity towards her fellow human beings. After reading this book, I think you will agree that the death of this kind, self-sacrificing and tenacious woman is an incalculable loss to the many, many people whose hearts she touched throughout her life. And I know that the beautiful words given to her by her devoted husband will touch your hearts as well.

On his deathbed our eponymous ancestor, Tūāhuriri, left us with these words: 'Atawhai ki te iwi—care for the people'. These words ask us to be more than polite hosts at a dinner party. We are asked to show compassion for our neighbours and for people we do not know. We are asked not to turn away from people we see suffering. Farid extols a similar lesson, and one that is all the more acute given the circumstances that have motivated his teaching it. He implores us to choose love over hate, compassion over negligence, understanding over ignorance. And, most remarkably, most challengingly—having publicly forgiven his wife's killer—he urges us to exercise forgiveness as a pathway to peace.

Farid writes that 'goodness is a constant work in progress', a work with which I believe this eminently poised and wise book can help us all. I feel greatly honoured to have been asked to contribute some opening remarks to this extraordinary story of love, compassion and forgiveness.

Professor Mohamad Abdalla, Director of the Centre for Islamic Thought and Education, University of South Australia

It is an absolute honour to write a foreword to Farid Ahmed's amazing book.

This is because, despite the massive tragedy faced by Farid—the loss of his beloved wife and 50 other friends and community members—he mustered the courage to forgive the killer, and to break the cycle of hate.

I visited Christchurch two days after the attack, and again in May 2019. I met with survivors and families of victims, and I witnessed the trauma and devastation they are dealing with and the sorrow that has come over them. Undoubtedly, the wounds inflicted on the Muslim community and New Zealand shall remain. However, the grace of the survivors and families, and their genuine desire to show love and compassion, speaks volumes about their strength of character. Choosing to break the cycle of hate is incredibly powerful.

Farid Ahmed was able to respond to hate with love, to revenge with forgiveness, and to anger with compassion. In forgiving the killer, he has adopted a moral stance that is supported by the teachings of Islam. Forgiving (*'afu* in Islam) the act of murder is a valid option for families of victims. The legal, moral and ethical validity for *'afu* is premised on both Islam's scriptures and the consensus of the scholarly community (*ijma'*). The Quran advocates for forgiveness as the best option (3:159 and 24:22, for example). The Prophet Muhammad (peace be upon him) advised, 'God elevates the position of a person who forgives.' (Book of Sahih Muslim) This advice serves as a rebuttal of the claim that those who forgive are cowardly and weak.

Most certainly, Farid's noble actions are a testimony to his courage, strength and moral uprightness. In essence, they are a testimony to his humanity.

To honour the life of his wife, Husna—and all other victims—Farid endeavours to engage with people in New Zealand and abroad to build bridges of understanding. In the scholarly community, we know that intercultural contact and the sharing of knowledge are the most powerful means of breaking down prejudice, stereotypes and Islamophobia. Breaking those barriers is exactly what Farid has been doing.

We also know that there is a clear relationship between the use of negative or exclusionary language and the incitement of hate and violence. The impact of this kind of language is not limited to Muslims; it affects everyone in society. Farid is obviously aware of this, as he always chooses to use positive and inclusionary language.

Farid's approach is one that we can all learn from. Politicians and members of the media, whose words have reach in our society, must learn from Farid's example. Their words can be powerful mechanisms of manipulation, discrimination and demagogy—or powerful mechanisms of change.

Farid's personal narrative debunks the stereotype that Muslims are violent people whose values are contradictory to Western values. His passionate story teaches us that objective, unbiased and less sensationalist language can help people—especially the most vulnerable—to find their place in society.

This book is a must-read for all of us, and is particularly important during this time of heightened tension between nations and peoples; a tension inflamed by negative rhetoric against the 'other'. Farid's story, his work, and the way he is choosing to deal with the loss of his beautiful wife, Husna, will surely touch the lives of all those he reaches.

Professor Mark Compton AM GCStJ,
Lord Prior of the Order of St John

The tragedy that struck on 15 March 2019 at al-Noor and Linwood mosques in Christchurch was impossible to adequately describe, let alone understand. It is hard to contemplate that any good could possibly come from such an evil event—which is what I thought, until I met Brother Farid Ahmed and heard his story and Husna's story.

I have the privilege of being the Lord Prior of the Order of St John worldwide and the Chairman of St John International. The Order is an ancient one, with its origins dating back to the 11th century in Jerusalem, where Benedictine monks established a hospital to care for pilgrims. In its modern form, St John operates in about 40 countries across the world, providing a range of services in healthcare and related areas. In New Zealand, St John Ambulance operates the emergency ambulance service for almost all of the country. It is one of the best ambulance services in the world.

On that fateful day in March 2019, St John paramedics were called to the al-Noor and Linwood mosques. They did an amazing job, showing great courage in the face of danger and unbelievable human devastation, while providing excellent and compassionate care to the victims of the shooting attack.

When I had the opportunity to make an official visit to New Zealand, I specifically asked if I could visit al-Noor and meet with the elders of that community in order to pay my respects, offer condolences on behalf of St John and stand with a community of Muslims as a member of a Christian-based organisation.

From the first moment, Brother Farid struck me with his centredness, his calm and tranquil state and his warmth. Very soon after our conversation started, he made the extraordinary revelation that, despite the tragedy of losing his much-loved wife and so many friends, he forgives the person who perpetrated this crime.

Two central tenets of the world's great religions and of those who live principled lives are unconditional love for one another and the ability to forgive. Farid Ahmed is a shining example to us all: even in the face of such terrible personal loss he can resolve to forgive, to continue to love and to look for what benefits might rise from the ashes of tragedy.

Husna's Story is a story of great love, great tragedy and great forgiveness. But it is also a reminder to us all that no matter what our beliefs—no matter what diverse backgrounds we might come from—those central tenets of unconditional love for one another and the ability to forgive make us stronger and better as individuals and as communities. Farid Ahmed has already taught me much, and the readers of *Husna's Story* will be stronger and better for sharing the lives of Farid and Husna and their family and friends.

Preface

I AM GOING TO TELL you a story. It is a story of love and of life, but it is also necessarily a story of hate and death.

This is the story of my beloved wife, Husna Ahmed, and her life. In it you will learn what kindness, bravery, generosity and wisdom look like, because Husna was a role model in all of these ways.

It is also the story of her death, which was the product of hate. From this tragedy, you will see a hero emerge: my wife, who responded to the hatred of her killer with love. Until her dying moment, she chose love, always and above all.

Finally, it is a story of forgiveness. Like my wife, I choose love. I have answered this killer's hatred with my own love, and I have forgiven him. I cannot condone his actions. What he did broke my heart, and grievously wounded so many people. It scarred our Muslim community, our city, our whole country. We will never go back to before, but we can choose love and forgiveness for the future. We should, if we wish to prevent anyone else suffering the loss that I and so many others have experienced because of one man's hate.

Although this is a story of tears, it is also a story of hope. There is so much hate in our world. Sometimes, it might even seem as though that's all there is—but it is not. Above all, there is love, always. Love is divine. Love survives. Love lives within us all, no matter what hardship or harm we face.

We do not need more hate in this world. What we need is love, and so that is my message. Let us choose love, not hate.

When I first learned that my wife had been killed, my heart crumbled and my whole world felt as though it had been thrown off balance. I floundered in my grief and shock, but my faith was there for me. I prayed to my Lord Allah and He guided me to be patient, He showed me the way back to the light. I realised that I had been given an opportunity: to spread a message of love to everyone I possibly could. I want that message of love to travel far and wide—from my home city of Christchurch to the edges of New Zealand and into the waters, to be dispersed all over the world. There is no limit to how far we might spread this message.

People are hungry for love, and they have already taken up this message as their own. I have seen it through the love that has been shown by so many people since my wife was killed.

If we all choose love, we can change the world together.

If Husna was capable of choosing love, and if I can do it, then I know you can too. We all can. The power rests within our hearts, just waiting for us to use it.

MY NAME IS FARID AHMED. I was born in 1962 in a village in Bangladesh, one of six siblings, with loving and well-respected parents. Our family lived on a farm, and we were nourished by sunshine and fresh fish and homegrown vegetables. I spent much of my childhood running about with my neighbourhood playmates. From the start, my parents taught me and my siblings to work hard and honestly for our daily needs, and to serve our fellow humans with wisdom, kindness and generosity. They instilled these values so deeply in me that I carry them to this day.

As a student, I always did my best, and even set about teaching myself English from an early age, though I wasn't yet quite sure why—back then, when I was so young, I could never have imagined that I would one day live in the faraway land of Aotearoa. At Sylhet Polytechnic Institute in Bangladesh, I studied engineering, and was active in student life and leadership. All the while, I did my best to be guided by the caring and loving principles my parents had taught me. With time, I discovered New Zealand, and decided I would like to call that peaceful place home.

I first arrived in New Zealand on 23 December 1988, at the age of 26. The moment I stepped off the plane in Auckland and filled my lungs with fresh air, I immediately felt a connection with the land beneath my feet. It was a strange and powerful feeling.

Inside the airport, I made friends with a Samoan man who lived in Manurewa, a suburb in the south of New Zealand's largest city.

'Do you know anyone in New Zealand?' he asked me. 'Do you have any family here?'

'No,' I said.

'Well, come with me,' he said. 'Come back to my place.'

So I followed my new friend back to his home, where his family welcomed me like I was a long-lost relative.

'Here is your room, brother,' he told me when he showed me into his house. 'You can stay with us for as long as you need.'

It didn't matter to him or his family that I was a stranger. They loved me regardless, saw me as their brother without needing to know everything about me. They let me know that their home was also mine.

At first, while my spoken English was still quite poor, I struggled to find suitable work in New Zealand. My engineering qualification was not of much use in this country. However, I did not let that hold me back, and I found work that I could do to support myself. Soon I was also looking into further study. I have always been a caring person, so it made sense for me to pursue a caring profession, and that is how I found homeopathy. Seven years and two diplomas later, I emerged with New Zealand's highest possible qualification in homeopathy and am a practising homeopath to this day. I am grateful for my profession, which allows me to comfort and care for others. I enjoy what I do.

In the more than three decades that I have lived here in New Zealand, my connection with this land has only deepened. Now, the earth of this country holds my wife, my older brother and my wife's older brother. They are a part of this land, as am I. This land is a part of me.

I love my adopted country. When I came here from Bangladesh, the people of New Zealand opened their arms to me, welcomed me as their brother. This country made room for me to live, work and study. It provided me and my family with the space to grow in peace. It welcomed my wife too, and it is where our daughter, Shifa, was born. It is our home, and we are its people.

However, when Husna and I had been married more than two decades, a man came to this country carrying hate in his baggage. On 15 March 2019, he armed himself as though for war, and he stormed into two Christchurch mosques and allegedly murdered and maimed innocent worshippers. He sought to destroy the peacefulness that is the bedrock of our country and of our faith, but he failed. That day, 51 people were killed, my beloved wife among them, but our Muslim community and our New Zealand responded to this hate with love. The wounds he inflicted on us will always remain, but we banded together and showed that peace is possible even after the very worst has happened. Our loving country is still a loving country.

I love New Zealand's people as I love every human: wholly and unconditionally. Based on the teachings of my faith, I believe that we are all part of a big family—the family of humankind. We are all brothers and sisters. Of course, even though we are family, each of us is unique. We are different from one another in so many ways. We come from different places, look different, speak different languages, practise different religions or don't practise any at all, believe different things, align ourselves with different communities and ideas. These differences are precious. They exist so that we may learn from one another. They are not there to divide us, or to drive us to hate and kill one another.

In order to achieve peace and happiness, humanity needs to embrace its differences and unite in love. My city, Christchurch, is also sometimes called the Garden City, and in gardens we can find an example of how our human family might live peacefully together. Each human is unique, just like every flower in a garden. This diversity is what gives the garden its beauty, making it a rainbow of colour and variation, beautiful to regard and to be a part of.

We have a choice about whether we embrace our differences or fear them. If we want to live peacefully, just as the flowers do, we need to see our differences as the wonderful and valuable things they are.

There is one path to unity for humankind, and it is paved with love and forgiveness. It is not paved with hate, or unkindness, or anger. The answer to hate is not more hate.

The answer is love.

The answer is peace.

The answer is forgiveness.

THIS BOOK BEARS TESTAMENT TO my divine love for my wife, Husna. During her life she was an inspiration to me and to so many others, and through her story she can continue to inspire us all to be more loving and forgiving. Husna embodied the very best qualities a person can have. She was a hero.

This book is also a tribute to all those whose lives were taken from them on 15 March 2019, by the same man who took the life of my wife. Like my wife, they too were heroes.

Everyone who has been a part of this book—and that includes you, as the reader who now holds it—is an active ambassador for spreading the message of love and forgiveness, for the peace and happiness of humankind. I cannot thank you enough, and I offer you my prayers from the bottom of my heart.

Please, spread this message far and wide. It is good work. The best work.

As a final note, should you find any error in this story, please know that it is a product of my own shortcomings, not of any ill will.

Please, read this story in the spirit in which it is offered to you: with love, with compassion and with forgiveness.

FARID AHMED
MARCH 2020

I

Days like any other

1.

One Monday

MY WIFE OFTEN FELT THINGS, saw things in her dreams, things that would eventually come to pass. Husna was always a spiritual person. Before we were married, before she had even accepted my proposal, she dreamed of me as both her husband and her father. It was a strange dream, and at first she couldn't understand it. But, eventually, she let the dream guide her into our marriage, a union that would prove to be happy and full of love, but would be cut short by one person's cruelty.

Sometimes, Husna's dreams caused her worry. When we had been married for a few years, she began to be plagued by dreams of something awful happening, nightmares that gave life to her worst fears. At the time, I had no idea that she was having these dreams, but her worry was obvious to me. Day by day, her concern grew, until I began to feel concerned too, without knowing why.

Why was she praying to Allah for my safety? What was she imagining might happen?

At the time, our lives were good in every sense. We were living in Nelson, we both had decent jobs, lots of friends, and plenty of time together. We were enjoying contributing to our community—running weekly Quran classes, teaching children on Sundays together, helping other families here in New Zealand and abroad, and always making an effort to invite newcomers into our home. And yet, Husna worried.

I did not know exactly what she was worrying about until much later. All I knew was that she was behaving strangely. If I arrived home even a few minutes late, she'd run to greet me. 'You're home!' she'd cry, obviously relieved, and I'd say, 'Of course I am. What is wrong? Why do you look so anxious?' but she wouldn't tell me. Later, I would learn that she was haunted by the certainty that something bad was going to happen—specifically, that something bad was going to happen to *me*.

This certainty that something awful was lurking just ahead in our future made her cling to me, as though she were desperate to keep me safe by sticking to me, as though she could fend off her fears simply by standing in their way. I could feel her fear growing—even if I didn't know what was driving it—and it made me uncomfortable.

Soon I, too, was praying to Allah, but I was asking for help. I could see that, in the process of trying to protect me, she had also turned me into her place of safety. I was both the site of her fears and the place where she sought comfort from them. I worried that the two would eventually collide, and her place of safety would be shattered. What would happen then?

I did what I could to calm her, to try to quell her fears. I reassured her that all we could do was pray, for our faith tells us we cannot control whatever is to be our fate, only how we respond to it.

And, alas, it was only a matter of time until Husna's worst fear came to pass.

EARLY ONE MONDAY IN 1998, I got up and said my morning prayer, then had my breakfast, before getting dressed for work. I grabbed my bag and said goodbye to Husna, wishing her peace for the day ahead. It was a day like any other. The sun was shining, the birds were singing, the road outside our house was busy with people going to and fro on their daily errands.

After I left, Husna said her own prayers. I worked at a nearby halal slaughterhouse, which was only a hundred metres from our home, so I had set off on foot, and Husna knew that I would have been reciting some memorised chapters from the Quran on my way. It's what I did every morning.

As Husna was getting ready to head off to work herself, there came a knock at the door. *Who could that be?* Husna wondered. She wasn't expecting anyone, and it was unusual to receive a visitor at that time on a weekday morning.

Then she heard a man's voice calling her name. His voice was loud, and something about the tone of it made her heart beat a little faster. Why did he sound like that? Had something happened?

He kept knocking, his voice growing louder, and Husna's fear grew too. A very bad feeling began to seep into her heart, black and thick like tar.

My husband . . . Is he OK?

Cautiously, she approached the door. Through the glass, she could see a man from my work—he was wearing a uniform the same as mine. That bad feeling engulfed her. It erased every other emotion and thought within her.

She opened the door.

The man broke down in tears. He was struggling to speak through his sobs, but it was clear he had something to say, something he desperately needed to tell Husna.

Seeing the man's distress, Husna felt her own fear vanish. She suddenly felt calm, and found herself assisting him to get his words out.

'It's your husband,' the man finally managed to say. 'He's been run over. By a car. They've taken him to the hospital in an ambulance.'

In that moment, Husna's nightmares became reality, but she had no time to cry or to feel sad. She simply had to respond. Afterwards, she told me, 'Whenever I face something truly terrible, I become like iron. I feel strong. I do not cry. I can cry alone, later, when the crisis is dealt with.' Others might have found themselves overcome or breaking down in such a terrifying situation, but not Husna. She met this awful news as she did any other hardship in her life: head on, with courage and strength. My wife always faced adversity bravely, wisely, calmly. It is a rare and precious gift to be able to do such a thing.

Husna gathered her things and rushed straight to Nelson Hospital. She arrived just in time to accompany me into the operating theatre. Again, she was clinging to me, but this time it was with a strength even I had not realised resided within her. I had known my wife was strong, but I had never truly seen how deep her courage ran. When she told me afterwards about how I had been, the state of my broken body, I could barely listen. It was horrifying, and yet she'd had to stand there and witness it all.

'I was so close to you when it happened,' she used to say to me afterwards. 'That car hit you so close to our home, and I was inside and had no idea. How could I have been unaware of something so awful happening to you, *priyō*, when I was so close by? *Amar dukkho holo je, ato kache thekeo amar volovashar pattroke sahajoo korte parlamna*,' she added with tearful eyes. *My sorrow is that, being so close, I could not help the person I love.*

HERE IS WHAT HAD HAPPENED. As I crossed the road on my way to work, I stopped to wait on the median strip, and a car hurtled into me at almost a hundred kilometres an hour. The road was in an 80-kilometre zone, but the driver was drunk, trying to overtake three cars, and driving so fast that I never saw him until it was too late. Bystanders said I was flung high into the air by the force of the impact, then came plummeting down to land on the car's windscreen, before my crumpled body slid on to the road. In his panic, and in his intoxicated state, the young man behind the wheel then accidentally drove the car over the top of me.

When I had first arrived at Nelson Hospital, the medical team performed X-rays and found that the bones in my legs had been shattered, so the physicians rushed me into surgery to reconstruct my tibias. They gave me a spinal anaesthetic, but my body began to swell, puffing up to the point that my chest rose above my chin.

Meanwhile, Husna stood by, watching the horror unfold, praying and hoping for the best, whispering to me to stay strong as I lapsed in and out of consciousness. She was all alone, without anyone to support or help her. She was still relatively new in this country, still learning the language and unfamiliar with complex medical terms. The person who would have supported her was me, and I was lying crushed and fighting for my life on an operating table. Yet, even as I faded, she held fast to her courage and her hope. Her resilience at a time of such stress remains an inspiration to me all these years later.

Husna asked the doctors to call my GP in Nelson, who was also a qualified homeopath. My wife wanted to ask her whether there was a homeopathic remedy they could try, even if only to help ease my pain, but the hospital staff brushed off the suggestion. 'That will never work,' they said. 'He needs more than that.' Husna repeated her request, but to no avail.

The decision was made by my medical team to transfer me to Christchurch Hospital, so I was loaded into a small plane and flown south to the Garden City. Husna followed in another plane the next morning. She arrived only to be greeted by news more terrifying than she could have imagined: I was in an induced coma, and according to my doctors had only a seven per cent chance of ever waking up again.

'Go home and find another husband,' one doctor told Husna callously. 'He is not going to live.'

But that doctor underestimated my wife.

Husna did not go home. She did not look for another husband.

The way she saw it, she still had a husband, and he needed her now more than ever.

Did she give up? She did not.

Did she break down crying? She wept, but she was not broken.

My wife was determined to remain beside me, to do whatever was humanly possible to turn things around. She believed that she had to do her very best, then put her faith and trust in Allah. She knew that she would need to be resilient, and would need to work hard, but she did not shy away from her task for a moment.

Husna held fast to me, strong and sure as an anchor. She stayed true to her marriage vows, praying for me, talking to me even while I lay unresponsive. She sought every scrap of information possible from the nurses and doctors attending to me. She sacrificed her well-being for my sake, giving up her own sleep and comfort to stay with me at the hospital.

I often wonder how I might have acted if things had been the other way around, and I cannot honestly know that. I am sure, however, that I would have always come in second to Husna's efforts. She did more than I ever could have, more than most people would, and she did it all because that was who she was.

A GOOD FRIEND FROM NELSON, Paul, sent a friend of his called Lesley to help Husna out. Lesley was kind and caring, and also a practising homeopath. At last, Husna thought she might have a chance to try some homeopathic remedies, to see if they might complement the doctors' medical treatments.

Several months earlier, Husna had ended up in Nelson Hospital herself, awaiting surgery to drain the fluid from a Bartholin's cyst.

Ahead of her surgery, I had given her one of my homeopathic remedies. When she was wheeled into the operating theatre, the surgeon had discovered that the fluid in the cyst had disappeared, and surgery was no longer necessary. So, as I lay there in Christchurch Hospital, deep in a coma which none of my doctors expected I would wake from, Husna thought that homeopathy might help. At the very least, she preferred to do something rather than simply sit by and watch me die.

The doctors in the hospital, however, were concerned about any possible adverse side-effects. They agreed to let her and Lesley try, but first made Husna sign a disclaimer to confirm that, should anything go wrong, she would take sole responsibility. She signed it, and fourteen days after my accident I woke up.

It had all paid off—Husna's love and steadfastness, the homeopathy, and the hard work of the doctors and nurses who had cared for me. I was out of danger. Given how poor my odds of survival had been, this was nothing short of a miracle. It brought a smile to everyone's face, and it filled formerly clouded hearts with bright hope.

However, I might have come out of the worst peril, but I had woken up to a new and drastically changed reality. When I had first arrived in Christchurch, the medical team had performed scans that had revealed the true extent of my injuries. That was when they realised that my spinal cord was bleeding, and that my back was broken.

IN THE FOURTEEN DAYS THAT she had stood by my side and slept on a couch next to my hospital bed, Husna had never given up her hope that I would be OK eventually. She believed that my stay in hospital would end sooner rather than later. She had not showered or eaten home-cooked food in those two weeks, and she was eager for us to go home to Nelson together. She was ready for us to resume our normal life.

However, when I woke up, it was clear that what was 'normal' for us had changed. A while after my accident, Husna confessed that she had noticed the wheelchair entrance when she'd first arrived at the hospital in Christchurch, and the thought had crossed her mind that I might end up in one. The notion had filled her with fear, so she pushed it away by holding on to the hope that it would never come to pass. She didn't let herself imagine the possibility again, but that only made it all the more heartbreaking for her when the doctor spelled it out for us.

'Mr Ahmed, you will never walk again,' he said. 'You will be in a wheelchair for the rest of your life. It is very important that you both accept this. It is the way things are now.'

This news, presented so starkly, left both Husna and me speechless for a few minutes. I couldn't think of anything to say. How does one respond to such life-changing news?

Then Husna spoke up. 'All that matters is that you are still alive,' she said to me. 'Don't worry. We will get through this together. I will help you.'

At first, I did not know what to do with her promise of help. If I am honest, in that moment, I was devastated, and Husna's offer only exacerbated that. I wanted to be able to take care of myself. I wanted to be able to take care of my wife. I did not know how I was going to be able to do that when I was suddenly so physically limited. I felt so weakened, as it seemed as though I had lost the capacity to be the man and the husband I believed I should be. How would I be able to give to my wife if I was always in need of her help? How would I provide for her? The thought of always being on the receiving end filled me with disappointment. However, there was nothing I could do or say, because the situation was outside of my control. All I could do was accept what was my destiny, and pray for the wisdom and courage to be able to do so graciously.

I was moved to Christchurch's Burwood Hospital for a six-month rehabilitation programme. In addition to my broken legs and back, I also had chest injuries, a concussion and extensive contusions. My rehabilitation was a long and trying journey. To begin with, I had nothing in my soul besides despair. Often, the side-effects of my injuries and medication were unbearable, a physical pain that paired with the anguish I felt inside.

Husna was right there beside me every minute, day and night. She kept a keen eye on the exercises I did, learning every step for herself, asking everything she could of the nurses, physiotherapists and doctors so that she could continue to support me when I came home again. One doctor would roll his eyes whenever he saw her, teasing her by saying, 'You again! What are you doing still here? The man needs some space!' Husna would smile in reply, but no amount of joking could unstick her from my side, and I was glad of it. I never got sick of being with Husna, nor she with me.

It was Husna who got me through that dark time. She constantly encouraged me to keep trying harder, and she consoled me whenever I felt overwhelmed. Her smiles, hugs and unwavering, unconditional love were a gift from God. Allah gave me Husna, my guardian angel. She was unfailingly positive, and it was her loyalty and support that carried me through that long rehabilitation and eventually got me home again.

To this day, I often think of what Husna endured in the wake of my accident. She did it all without complaint, and with a smile on her face. I had already thought my wife was an incredible woman, but it was in those difficult months that I truly appreciated just how exceptional she really was. She was my rock, and her devotion during that time is carved indelibly on to my heart. No amount of time will ever fade the memory of her selflessness and love. The more I think about it, the more it moves me.

I wonder how she felt in the days when she was alone by my side, praying and hoping that I would wake up again. What must she have thought? What must she have felt? Trying to fathom the sorrow, anxiety, fear and helplessness she must have experienced fills me with pain. I wish I could have shouldered that agony for her, and yet I was the source of it. I wish that it could have been me who had endured that hardship, wish that I could have saved her at least some of the suffering that life held for her.

THE YOUNG MAN WHO GOT drunk and then got behind the wheel of his car never apologised for the consequences of his reckless actions. When he drove into me and then ran me over, he altered the course of my life, and of Husna's. The accident led to irreparable damage, but it also sowed the seeds of future good, even if it wasn't possible to see it in the immediate aftermath.

Learning lies within even the most horrible tragedy, and Husna showed me how to find the way towards knowledge by following the path lit with love and forgiveness. In the early days after I awoke from my coma, our talk inevitably turned to the man who had hit me.

'He must have had a bad day, the poor guy,' Husna said, without hesitation.

It didn't matter that he never said sorry or showed any remorse. Husna forgave him anyway. That was just who she was. She never held a grudge.

And, by showing forgiveness to a person whose actions had caused us so much pain, she showed me how to do the same.

Husna showed me how to love, and how to forgive.

2.
One Friday

I HAVE NEVER BEEN MUCH of a morning person. Husna was always the early riser in our house. Where she never had any problem getting up early, I have always struggled to get myself going at the start of the day. Husna was my human clock, my early bird. By contrast, I was the lazy one—after my morning prayer, I loved to take a nap, especially on the weekend. The morning of Friday 15 March 2019 was no exception: I got up and said my morning prayers then went back to my room to rest a while.

From there, I could hear the sounds of a normal weekday morning—the clatter of cupboards opening and drawers sliding shut as Husna prepared breakfast for our fifteen-year-old daughter.

'Quickly, Shifa, eat your breakfast,' I could hear her urging.

'Have you got your bag? Where are your books?'

Husna couldn't help herself. Her maternal instinct took over and made her hurry our daughter along, even though Shifa didn't need hurrying.

I could hear them chirping away at each other like two little birds. They were always chatting, those two, and never more so than at the kitchen table. It became a hot-talk table when they sat at it together. Chatterboxes, both of them. It made me smile to hear their words dancing in the air, tumbling out in the excitement of everything they had to share with one another, and I said a quiet prayer, thanking Allah for giving me such a happy family and asking for their safety.

Then I heard bustling as they gathered their things and made their way out of the house. The door slammed behind them, and all was silent.

They had taken their chatter into the car, and I knew they would still be talking as much as ever as they headed towards Shifa's school. Husna had always insisted that we drive Shifa to school; she did not want Shifa to walk. This was a brilliant idea on my wife's part, as it gave us a guaranteed segment of time at the beginning and the end of the day during which we could teach Shifa something. In the short time it took to drive between our home and her school, Shifa could memorise Quranic verses and we could answer her questions and talk to her. Husna wanted us, as parents, to do as much as we could to instil in our daughter the maturity she'd need to navigate her adult life. It was usually Husna who drove Shifa, but if she was ever busy or sick the task fell to me.

'Don't forget you have to pick up Shifa,' Husna would say to me on those days. 'You remember what time you need to leave, don't you?'

'Yes, *priyō*,' I would reply. 'I remember, because you have already reminded me several times.'

She would go quiet for a while . . . until she asked me again.

In October 2018, Husna had to undergo serious surgery to treat her Crohn's disease, and ended up in hospital for some time afterwards. When she eventually returned home, she was still recovering and tired. So, for a few months, it was me who dropped off and picked up Shifa, and Husna was not happy about it. She worried about my health, and fretted about the demands that driving so much would place on me, not sparing a thought for her own healing. She tried to start driving again sooner than she had been advised to, but I told her not to. She needed to let herself recover fully, I said, and she agreed—albeit reluctantly. She had started driving again in February and, at least to begin with, I insisted we take turns: since she was such a morning person, Husna could do the drop-off, and I would pick Shifa up.

Often, Husna wouldn't come home afterwards, instead staying out and about on various errands, but on this particular Friday she did come straight home. I knew the minute she'd returned, because the house filled with noise once again. Husna was always busy, always doing several things at once. She was very active in our community, giving her time to those who needed it. I heard her head into the kitchen, then the sound of taps running and knives chopping as she set about preparing food for the day ahead. While she cooked, she talked on one of the two phones she always had beside her, caught up in first a conversation with one of the

Bangladeshi ladies she was helping, then in another about some of her volunteer work. If she wasn't talking on a phone, she was about to silence one's ringing by answering it.

Once she finished cooking, Husna turned her attention to getting ready for Jumu'ah, or Friday prayers, just as I began to do the same. Friday is a very significant day for us as Muslims. We believe that it was on a Friday that God created the first man, Adam, and that Adam and Eve descended to earth from heaven on a Friday. We also believe that the world will end and the resurrection will take place on a Friday. As a result, Jumu'ah is one of the most exalted Islamic rituals, compulsory for every able Muslim man and optional for Muslim women. Jumu'ah is the largest weekly gathering for our community, and consists of two parts: first a sermon, which imparts advice from the Holy Quran and the Prophet's teachings (peace be upon him), then joint prayer in rows behind the imam. Husna and I never missed Jumu'ah unless we were too sick to attend, for we always left with a sense of peace, tranquillity and spiritual satisfaction.

While she dressed, Husna carried on taking calls. Busy, busy, busy—and yet she still somehow managed to be ready before I was.

'We need to leave in ten minutes,' Husna reminded me, and I nodded and tried to go faster. Sometimes, since my accident, I feel as slow as a snail, and this was one of those days.

'Oh, and remember that you need to take those homeopathic remedies with you. One of the ladies just called to remind me about hers.'

Husna's ability to multitask never ceased to amaze me. Not only was she able to co-ordinate getting our daughter out of the door and off to school at the same time as taking care of the cooking and fielding calls about her community work, but she also managed to remember the things that I needed to do for my homeopathy practice. It was all business as usual for her. Husna would often relay to me requests for homeopathic remedies from the Bangladeshi or Muslim ladies she knew, and the two of us formed a smooth and reliable team. It was not her job to do so, but she did it because she cared about others—and, also, because she was very good at it. She was something of a taskmaster.

'Time to go,' Husna said. 'Are you ready?'

But I wasn't. After all these years, I'm very used to my wheelchair, but even so it can hamper me in tasks that would be incredibly simple for an able-bodied person. It doesn't just slow me down; sometimes it can bring me to a total stop. I didn't respond, and Husna noted my silence and came over to see what had absorbed my attention.

'Can I help?' she asked.

My sense of independence kept me tight-lipped, even though I did indeed need some help. Instead of replying, I zeroed in on the task before me. In my attempt to go faster, I had made a mistake while tying up a tassel on my trousers. I had tied the wrong knot, and now I couldn't get it undone. I stubbornly pulled and picked at it, but the harder I tried to loosen it the tighter the knot became.

Husna immediately saw exactly what was happening. She knew me so well—often better than I even knew myself. She looked at the awkward tangle of string, then at my big, clumsy fingers plucking at it, and she knew that I did not want to be defeated by a little knot. But then she looked at the time, and she saw that we were now running late. In that moment she weighed up her options, and she decided to come to my rescue. Ordinarily, if we hadn't been pressed for time, she would have given me the space I needed to sort things out for myself, because she understood how challenging just this sort of scenario could be for me. It wasn't just about the knot; it was about the fact that, since my body had slowed, my mind had quickened, and it was always a struggle to find a balance between the two extremes. Situations like my tussle with the knot only served to highlight how incompatible my limited body sometimes was with my independent mind.

Gently, she said, 'Would you like me to try?'

I nodded.

She leaped into action, her small and nimble fingers undoing the knot that my large ones had made. As she retied my tassel for me, she teased me good-naturedly.

'It's just a little knot,' she said. 'An easy thing to fix . . . No need to let something so small get the better of you. Lucky you have a wife with small hands to come and fix it for you!'

While her quick hands were busy tidying up my mess, her quick tongue was putting my bruised ego in its place. It was the sort of friendly competition we often engaged in, and today I had to hand the victory to her. She deserved it. Marriage requires compromise, and it often transpires that accepting a personal loss can lead to deeper love and trust.

Husna revelled in her win, smoothing down the untangled tassel with a flourish and smiling at me. It was as though she'd just been handed an Olympic gold medal, and seeing her pride I swallowed my own and smiled back at her.

'Congratulations!' I said. 'You win . . . for today.'

I will never forget her happiness in that moment. It shone from her face and encompassed me, dissipating any remnant of frustration that lingered in me. We were both so full of joy. After all, a victory for one of us was a victory for both of us, no matter how small.

SINCE WE HAVE ONLY THE one car, whenever Husna and I travelled together it was always me who drove. It was easier that way. In our car, a robot emerges from the boot to stow my wheelchair while I drive. When the car is parked, the robot extracts my chair again and puts it next to the driver's seat. So it was me who drove us to mosque. The trip usually takes about 25 minutes—plenty of time to cover a range of topics. As we set off, we both said a few prayers for our journey.

Then Husna said, 'Don't forget that we have to pick up Shifa at three-fifteen today.'

'Of course I won't, *priyō.*'

After our prayers, our conversation in the car would usually turn to whatever the topic of the day might be—often planning classes or social gatherings, or discussing family issues, or continuing whatever debate we might have last been having. It was in the car that we would share ideas and ask questions, and learn from one another through our conversations. Today was no different. I always loved talking with my wife. Usually, when I was driving, it was Husna who did most of the talking—but not because I'm not a talkative person. Instead, I used the opportunity to listen. Husna was an exceptional listener—my best listener—and driving the car always provided me with an opportunity to make sure that I listened to her in return. As well as being an important part of our marriage, listening was an important part of my job as a homeopath.

In 24 years of marriage, Husna and I travelled together in the car so many times. I cannot even begin to count the hours we spent talking to one another in just the same way we did on this Friday. Our car conversations—full of joy and sadness and everything in between—all blur and merge together so that it's impossible for me to extract one from another. Much like that little knot I struggled with, they've become completely bound up together, and I'd need Husna here with me to untangle the strands that we spoke of on that particular Friday.

I do remember that we were happy. We did not argue about anything, and we laughed together. We spoke of things we were looking forward to, of good deeds we still hoped to do. Our plans looked into the future, full of good intentions, and we were both on the same page—a team, as always. There was no dark cloud hanging over us, no hint of horror hiding up ahead. We were full of hope, resting in the belief that this was just one of many more car conversations we would share.

JUST AFTER 1 P.M. WE arrived at Masjid al-Noor on Deans Avenue in Christchurch, and I parked in my usual spot behind the mosque. It's a handy place—close to the rear entrance, near the walkway leading directly to the women's room. Since I am the only paraplegic worshipper at our mosque, everyone always leaves that parking spot for me.

As I prepared to get out of the car, Husna pulled out a bottle of scented *attar* oil and rubbed a bit of it on me. She'd already done so before we'd left the house.

'Husna! You're bathing me in the stuff!' I said.

She tutted playfully. She knew I was joking. 'I'm just making sure you are presentable,' she replied, as she rubbed some more on herself too. 'What would you do if you didn't have me here to take care of you?'

She often used to tease me by saying this.

'Here are your homeopathic remedies,' she said, passing them to me once I was out of the car and in my wheelchair. 'And, here, sit up just a little so that I can straighten out your clothes.'

I did as I was told, appreciative of her characteristic care about my appearance. She always made sure I looked (and smelled) my best. She then checked the stabilisers on my wheelchair. I had once forgotten to put them in place when I had headed out to a local shop, and had ended up flipped over on the footpath. Ever since then, Husna had been extra careful about them, my safety being as important to her as my good appearance.

'Do you have any meetings after mosque today?' she asked me.

'No, I have no meeting after prayer. Why are you asking?'

'I have a few things I need to do before we go and pick up Shifa. Remember we have to get her at—'

'Three-fifteen. Yes, I remember.'

She held out the car keys. 'Shall I keep these, or will you take them?'

'Let me take them. You're usually later out of mosque than I am on Fridays.'

'OK, then.' She looked at me as though she were thinking about whether there was anything else she needed to say, and then she smiled at me. Husna was always smiling. 'Would you like me to help you get inside?' she said as we reached the back entrance to the men's room.

'No, no. I will be fine,' I assured her. 'Don't worry about me. I will see you afterwards.'

So Husna headed inside Masjid al-Noor, towards the women's and children's room.

Neither of us knew it then, but it was the last time that we would see one another in this world.

II

Husna

3.

Wisdom

বিজ্ঞতা

WHEN SHE WAS BORN, THE woman who would one day become my beloved wife was named Husne Ara Tajmin. After we were married, we decided that her name would be Husna Ahmed. We made this decision together—we wanted her name to take its Arabic form, and we also wanted to simplify our names so that we both had just a first name and a surname.

In Islam, names matter. They must be meaningful, and will often represent the bearer's personality. According to the teachings of Islam, every human born on this earth is an ambassador of God, and their name should reflect that high honour. When a person calls another by their name, they show their respect through that name. For this reason, it was very important to both Husna and me to choose a good name for her upon the occasion of our marriage.

So what does Husna mean? In Bengali, it means *uttom* or 'the best'. It is an Arabic word, and is mentioned a few times in the Holy Quran. For example, we are advised to talk to others with *husna*, meaning kindly, nicely, politely or justly (2:83). Elsewhere, Allah's names are described as *asmaaul husna*, or 'most beautiful' (59:24), and we are advised to accept what is *husna* or 'the best' (92:6). The more general definition of *husna* is 'good deed' or 'good qualities', and the latter is what it means when used as a name. There could not have been a more fitting name for my wife. There was so much about Husna that was good.

As for our surname, Ahmed means 'the one who should be praised'. The Holy Prophet Muhammad (peace be upon him) had the name Ahmed for his praiseworthy character, and this inspired Husna to take what was already my surname as her own. We both wanted the same surname. As her husband, the man who has known her for the past 24 years, I can say without a moment of hesitation that my wife had a praiseworthy character. Her family, who knew her even before I did, would say the same, as would her friends and everyone else who knew her.

Husna embodied her names. She contributed positively, in every way she could, to the lives of those around her. She touched so many hearts through her praiseworthy character. Her passion for helping others and her ability to put others' needs ahead of her own was inspirational, not just to me but to the many, many people who knew and loved her.

The world needs more people like my wife.

HUSNA WAS BORN WITH A smile on her face, or so I have been told.

She came into this world, healthy and happy, on 10 December 1974. She was born in Zangal Hata, a village in Bangladesh surrounded by lush tropical greenery. Zangal Hata is in Golapganj, a district on the outskirts of the city Sylhet, in eastern Bangladesh. Bangladesh is around the same size as the North Island of New Zealand, but is home to over 160 million people. It is one of the most densely populated countries in the world, and as a result many who live there—including Husna—soon learn that they'll have to work hard if they wish to earn good fortune in life.

Sylhet is known as a spiritual city. Its residents are inclined towards religiosity and are very hospitable, welcoming strangers as guests into their homes and feeding them lavishly. It is in the villages of Sylhet that the generosity tends to be most warmly extended. During the planting and harvesting seasons, villagers will work extremely hard, then invite family and relatives to many occasions throughout the rest of the year. Their generosity can be extravagant, for instance on special occasions such as weddings. It's therefore perhaps not very surprising that Husna, who grew up in just such a village, was so generous herself.

Zangal Hata has a few high hills, and the house that my wife grew up in happened to be on top of one of those hills. In 1997, when we had been married for three years, we returned to her village for a visit and Husna led me up the 50 or so steps (although it felt like many more) to her family home. It was a hard workout for me, but at the top Husna was as fresh-faced and full of energy as she had been at the bottom.

As I stood in the yard and caught my breath, I looked down at the red sandy soil. It was so different from the soil in my own home town just over 20 kilometres away. Here, the soil didn't hold the rain after a downpour and the resulting dryness meant it was an inhospitable place for mosquitoes—unlike where I grew up. I was very happy about the absence of mosquitoes. That night, I slept without a mosquito net, and even all these years later I can still remember what a freedom that felt, to sleep uncovered and unbitten in Bangladesh.

Husna's family had been living in this village for generations, and had made many contributions to the prosperity of their community. Her father, Noor Uddin, was a village leader who owned a grocery shop in the local market. He was a religious man, well known for his fairness in resolving disputes between villagers and for his honesty in business. Her mother, Zahanara Begum, was modest and well educated, and a very caring parent. Husna was the youngest of five siblings—she had two brothers and two sisters. As the baby of the family, Husna received a lot of attention and love from her parents, from her older siblings and from her relatives. Born into a safe, secure, well-respected family and blessed with loving parents, things looked good for baby Husna.

However, although she was born smiling, it was not long before hardship came into her life. When Husna was just eight months old, her mother died. Zahanara had become ill just a few months after her youngest daughter's birth, and it was a sickness that was cruel and, ultimately, deadly.

Suddenly, everything in Husna's happy family home was inverted. Where once there had been joy, there was now grief. Her mother's love had been replaced by a cold absence. Relatives swiftly appeared, eager to help, especially with caring for baby Husna. They wanted to rear her, to adopt her, to give her the motherly love that she had lost. But Husna's father could not accept these offers of help if they meant his baby girl would be taken away. Still wading through his own thick grief, he decided to rear the baby himself.

Doing this took extraordinary courage. Furthermore, he decided not to marry again, instead dedicating his life to ensuring the security and comfort of his children. Noor became a full-time single parent, taking responsibility for all of the associated childcare tasks: feeding, carrying, cleaning, bathing, singing lullabies, telling bedtime stories. He used his savings to provide for his children and for their educations. I greatly admire everything my dear father-in-law did for his family. He was a very wise and loving father.

Although she was just a baby when her mother died, Husna felt the loss keenly. It was still painful to her. Of course, her father could never wholly replace her mother, but the resilience and devotion that Noor showed in the wake of his wife's death left its mark on his children. Husna saw in the example of her father how to be strong in the face of grief and calamity. He taught her how to transform sadness into positivity, through hard work.

Armed with the resilience that she had seen her own father wield, Husna grew up prepared to face the difficulties that awaited her in this life.

WHEN HUSNA WAS OLD ENOUGH, she began attending the local primary school. Like many children, she enjoyed school and she was good at her lessons. Husna might have lost her mother's love, but she gained her father's wisdom and soon grew into a mature and much-admired young woman.

One of the many things Husna's father taught her was how to communicate confidently with her elders. She easily related to her teachers, and knew how to manage her classmates. Before long, Husna had gained the respect and admiration of her teachers, and was even given the task of teaching a small group of her classmates. She was a natural leader and confident public speaker, and her teachers ensured she had the chance to exercise these skills at every opportunity. Always quick to pick up new things, Husna learned leadership skills that would serve her throughout the rest of her life.

My wife was very pretty, and she had an aura that drew others to her and made them feel comfortable in her presence. Part of her charisma lay in the attention she paid to her dress: she always took an enormous amount of care with her appearance, and presented herself immaculately. From primary-school age, she began wearing her headscarf. Furthermore, she never missed her prayers, even during school time. Her devotion to her faith and her self-discipline extended to all aspects of her life, and only added to the admiration her peers and elders held for her.

Her cheerful personality naturally lent itself to sports. Lean and always bursting with energy, Husna could run like the wind, leaving any competitors far behind her. There was no one faster than her. While she was at school, Husna won many prizes. In fact, from time to time, the school had to place a limit on the number of events that Husna could compete in, so that other kids could win too. Husna was so good that she used to win all the prizes!

There was one quality in Husna that stood out among all the

rest, and that was her exceptional moral character. She was a smart, pious young woman. Due to her maturity and confidence, her classmates respected her like an older sister.

HUSNA LEARNED TO WALK BY holding on to her father. For twelve years, she lived and learned in the shelter and safety of his care—but then her father passed away too.

'My whole castle collapsed,' Husna once told me, remembering how she felt when her father died. 'He was our everything.'

This time, Husna was old enough to feel the acute grief that comes with losing a parent. As well as loving her, Husna's father had been her guide, her guardian, her role model. And, in a more practical sense, he had provided her with life's necessities: food, clothes and education. Without him, Husna and her siblings were cut adrift. She told me she felt as though her world had shrunk in on itself. She felt alone. Orphaned. Her siblings, too, were grieving and confused. They did not know what to do. How were they going to survive?

Noor's death brought financial difficulties knocking at the family's door, but also relatives with offers of help. However, much like their father before them, Husna and her siblings resisted these offers, not least because the help was conditional. Husna believed it would be best to avoid those obligations. She wanted to stand strong, to do things for herself. 'Where there is a will, there is a way,' Husna used to say. 'Allah is looking after me.'

One of her older sisters, Rushna, was at college and not yet married. Rushna had inherited her father's strong personality, and she said to Husna, 'I will take care of you.'

But, in order to do so, Rushna would need money, so she found a job as a teacher's aide in a local high school. She also started a sewing business from home—a shrewd move. Rushna could already sew well, so she took a few lessons on cutting women's and girls' dresses and then got down to work—and she roped Husna in to help. The two sisters would work late into the night in order to meet their delivery dates, and very soon their little business had blossomed into a flourishing enterprise. They became well known for their honesty and efficiency, and their hard work forced the financial woes from their doorstep. Husna was proud to see how their struggle had paid off, turning dark times into bright ones.

The whole experience cemented the lessons that life had already begun teaching Husna. Her resilience solidified, and she saw in practice how hard work might transform one's fortunes. She learned how to embrace the struggle to improve her lot, instead of letting herself get waylaid by sadness and hopelessness. 'The opportunities are out there in the world,' Husna often used to say to me. 'We just need to see them, and use them.'

Life is full of hardship. There is no escaping it, and some of us might find ourselves beset by more of it than we would wish. The trick lies in how we respond to it, how we face the difficult things that happen to us. Husna never hid her hardships, often talking about them, but they did not define her. Instead, difficulty ignited my wife's determination, driving her to always strive to get above it, to the place where light and positivity shine. Whenever adversity arrived in Husna's life—which it did, and often—she would greet it with a smile. That bright smile hid a world of woe, but people meeting her for the first time would never have suspected it.

And therein lay the true beauty of my wife. No matter what life threw at her, she never lost her capacity to love, to be kind, to forgive. She put her resilience, wisdom and innate positivity to work transforming grief into a smile. In doing so, she became a role model to others, empowering them to do the same.

Husna always believed in the beauty of this world. 'Behind the clouds in the sky,' she would say, 'the sun is shining. It will come out again soon.'

4.

Trust

আস্থা

OFTEN, TOO MUCH CHOICE CAN pose as much of a problem as not enough. When a person has too many options to choose from, they can find themselves incapacitated. How is one to know which is the right choice, out of many, to make? The more options there are, the more complicated things become. This is precisely the dilemma that Husna faced when it came to marriage.

Thanks to her many exceptional qualities, Husna was viewed by many families as an extremely desirable daughter-in-law. Everyone, it seemed, wanted this clever, pious, hard-working and pretty girl to marry their son or their brother or their grandson. She had marriage proposals coming at her from every direction, but no parents alive to help her field them.

What's more, in Husna's culture, it is traditional for sisters in a family to marry in order of age. Husna was the youngest of three girls, and her older sisters were not yet married. She wanted them to be married before she was, but that didn't stop the proposals from coming. It was overwhelming.

There was, of course, also the matter of money. Many wealthy families wanted Husna as a bride, but their proposals always came with some form of financial expectation attached. How were Husna and her siblings ever to meet such expectations? Then there were some families who claimed not to care about the money, who said they would welcome her with no financial contribution on her part, but Husna was wary of such offers. She wasn't sure whether it would be wise to put too much trust in promises from strangers.

My wife also had an independent mind, and she was not keen to give up that independence too easily—or to just anyone. So, in her wisdom and maturity, she decided she would simply wait. She would wait until a potential groom came along who fully satisfied her heart. This was not an easy thing to do in her culture, but Husna had an iron will. She had guts. When she was pressured, she responded politely, calmly and with that smile of hers. My wife met aggression with gentleness, shaming the ugly behaviour of others.

The way Husna saw it, this was just one of life's many tests. All she had to do was pass it, as she had passed so many tests already. Husna stood her ground, and while she did, she prayed. Soon, her prayers were answered: her eldest sister was married, then her next sister was on her way to marriage too. The road was clear for Husna to get married.

HOWEVER, THAT WAS JUST THE first of many hurdles Husna would have to traverse on the road to her wedding day. She still had many proposals coming in—too many. As the days and weeks passed, more and more arrived. In Husna's family's tradition, it is common for families to seek cultural marriages for their children. Usually, the groom's family will send a proposal to the bride's family, as this shows the groom is genuinely seeking marriage with his family's involvement. Sometimes, a bride's family might propose to a potential groom, but it's not often the case, as families take a bride's reputation very seriously. If a groom's family begs for a bride, that is seen as a mark of respect.

Husna had proposals coming in from Bangladeshis at home and from all over the world. But, no matter how many came in, none clicked with Husna. She could not find one that she felt right about saying 'yes' to.

It's not uncommon for young people to desire the perfect spouse. They have a long list of ideals, and they will search far and wide for the person who will tick all of the boxes. This search can take years, and make the marriage process very difficult, sometimes even rendering it futile if the perfect person never appears. Husna herself had some very specific qualities in mind when it came to picking a groom. Later, when we were married, I would pester her, trying to get her to tell me just what sort of person she'd been hoping to find. She would not tell me everything, but she did share some of her secrets. 'I wanted to find someone who I knew I could trust,' she said, and would add that she knew she wanted to marry someone older than her. 'I grew up with my father,' she would explain. 'I am happy with older, wiser people.' She hoped her husband would be someone who could be a role model to her and to others, someone with a good reputation and who was well respected. Respect was important to Husna, particularly the mutual respect between a husband and wife. She was determined to find someone who valued respect, and also selflessness, as highly as she did.

What's more, independent Husna did not want to marry someone who thought they could boss her around—and, in our 24 years of marriage, I learned just how true this was! Rather, Husna wanted a husband who could guide her with his wisdom, and who would give her the freedom to do the things she cared about, namely helping others. She did not want, or need, to be ordered around.

What she knew she needed was love. Husna had already lost the love of first her mother and then her father, and she hoped a husband's love would go some way towards compensating for that. Love was incredibly important to my wife, and at times she would hold tightly to me, letting me carry her around or—after my accident—sitting on me while I pushed my wheelchair about.

Husna was not motivated by money. She cared more about all of the other qualities that I have mentioned than she did about living a life of luxury, but in many ways money might have been easier to find.

Nonetheless, Husna was adamant. The proposals kept coming in, and one by one she assessed and then rejected them. There was nothing that felt quite right.

Then, one day in 1992, a proposal arrived from the father of a Bangladeshi man who lived in New Zealand. For some reason, this one caught Husna's attention.

AFTER WE WERE MARRIED, I used to ask Husna to tell me how she'd felt when she had first received my proposal. My late father, Hafiz Mokarram Ali, had delivered it for me, going on my behalf to visit Husna and Rushna. Since Husna and I had grown up in towns so near to one another, we had met briefly, but by this time I was living in New Zealand. I had been reasonably well known and respected in my district, as was my father, but that didn't mean it was a given that she'd accept.

'Come on, Husna,' I'd press. 'Tell me! How did you feel when you got my proposal?'

'I felt a surprising calmness in my heart,' she would say. 'It was as though every box I had was being ticked without any effort on my part. My heart raced with joy, although I couldn't work out why. And my eyes shed tears, but it was sadness mixed with joy.'

At last, a proposal had come along that felt right, and Husna took this as a signal that we were meant to be together. She felt right about me, just as I felt right about her. Our love for one another was divine.

Husna accepted my proposal, and happily.

HUSNA MIGHT HAVE FOUND A husband at last, but she still had the wedding ahead of her. She later confessed to me that she was extremely nervous during this time. All manner of questions raced through her mind. *Will I like my husband?* she would wonder. *Will he like me? Will we be happy? Will we love each other?*

Round and round and on and on the questions went, bumping against one another inside her head. These are just the sort of concerns that any young person facing the prospect of marriage might have. Marriage joins two people with two different mindsets and from two different upbringings. Therefore, every marriage, no matter how well matched the couple might seem, is something of a gamble. Husna was all too aware that anything might happen to mar the happiness of a marriage. Plus she knew that, once you're married, you're stuck in that marriage for a good long time. It pays to choose wisely.

Little did Husna know that, at the same time, I was experiencing my own fair share of nerves, and they'd started before I'd even asked for her hand. I had always been very shy around girls, so asking one to marry me was always going to be an enormous challenge. It felt as though my reputation was on the line. It was, therefore, fortunate for me that I didn't have to actually make the proposal myself—my father did it for me, according to our family tradition. That meant I could hide behind him, so to speak, while I nervously waited to see how Husna would respond. When she did accept, my father welcomed her as his own daughter, integrating her into our family—and I breathed a sigh of relief. 'When you said yes, you saved my pride, Husna!' I used to joke with her afterwards.

But, just like Husna, I was also nervous as our marriage approached. Since childhood, I'd struggled with taking responsibilities seriously and I worried about how I would handle the duties of marriage. *What will my new wife expect of me?* I wondered. *Will I be able to fulfil her expectations . . . or will I let her down?*

After Husna had accepted my proposal, we began to communicate with one another under her family's supervision. We wrote letters back and forth, and also spoke on the phone. At the same time, back in Bangladesh, she and her family began visiting mine, so that my parents could get to know their future daughter-in-law better. It wasn't long before they were extremely fond of her. What they told me of her filled me with happiness, but the question still lingered: *What is she going to ask of me?*

Usually, in our culture, the two families involved will discuss expectations and make financial demands before a marriage. Sometimes, these demands lose all proportion, with families asking for exorbitant sums of money as insurance against anything going wrong in the marriage. But Husna and her family had asked for nothing, and nor had my family. Husna and I each wanted the same simple thing: a loving spouse.

It might seem that I should have let the matter rest at that. I could have simply been relieved that my bride had asked for nothing in terms of money from me and my family, but to tell the truth her lack of demands filled me with as much fear as it did love. It made me realise that my bride would be no ordinary wife— that in fact I had found a precious soul. What if I was not able to honour her nobility?

In truth, I knew I needed someone to motivate me, and it was looking as though Husna would do just that. She would spur me to be nobler myself. Our Prophet (peace be upon him) said, 'Most fortunate are the men who have righteous wives,' and I would find this to be true in my marriage to Husna. From before we were even married, I knew she loved me for me, and not for money.

THE ACTUAL FACT OF HOW we would get married posed another difficulty. Amid all the nerves and excitement of our marriage proposal, neither of us had given much thought to the logistics of the wedding. Normally, I would have been expected to go to Husna in Bangladesh, where we would marry, and then we would return to New Zealand together as husband and wife. It made the most sense this way—who, after all, would expect a young woman to leave the safety of her home to travel halfway around the world to marry a strange man in a strange land?

However, for a number of reasons at that time, it was impractical for me to travel so far. It was soon clear that me going to Bangladesh was not an option.

By the time we realised that getting married might not be as easy as we had hoped, however, Husna and I were well and truly stuck with each other. We knew we were meant for one another, and we did not want to give up on our dream of being together.

So I spoke to my father.

'I want to marry Husna,' I said, 'but I can't go to Bangladesh. Please, will you go to her family and ask them to arrange for her to come here to New Zealand? I will marry her as soon as she arrives. There's no other way.'

'Are you crazy, Farid?' My father was clearly disappointed in me for even asking such a thing of him. 'I cannot do that. There's no way that her family will agree.'

When I tried to make my pleas again, he shut the conversation down.

'I'm not doing it. I won't talk about it anymore,' he said.

I could see things from my father's point of view, and began to ask myself how I could have ever put such a request to him. I prayed to Allah for guidance, begging for His help.

Meanwhile, over in Bangladesh, Husna was waiting to hear

from me and my family. She had placed her trust in me, believing that I would ensure our marriage would go ahead. She was waiting, waiting, waiting.

There was nothing for it. I had to somehow find a way to get my father to carry out my request. I knew that I shouldn't ask him again, that what I was asking him to do compromised not just my reputation but his own, but I did not know what else to do. I was desperate.

'Please,' I said. 'Take my request to Husna's family. You can blame me. Please, just see what they say.'

So, reluctantly, my father went to them. Unsurprisingly, Husna's family was hesitant. My father was preparing to receive the firm 'no' he'd been expecting when Husna spoke up.

'Let me go to him,' she said to her family. 'I trust his integrity. He will not betray me.'

5.

Courage

সাহস

SO MY COURAGEOUS BRIDE-TO-BE FOLLOWED her heart, and she farewelled her family and her village, then boarded a plane to New Zealand. She arrived in Auckland in January 1994. It is difficult to fathom the bravery that coming here took: she was leaving behind everything and everyone she had ever known to embark, alone, on a journey that would alter the course of her life forever.

While Husna was en route, I was driving from my home in Nelson up to Auckland, in order to meet her at the airport. On the way, I stopped in Hastings to pick up a friend so he could attend our wedding. The weather was awful during the drive, and we got to Auckland several hours later than planned, at around three in the morning. When we arrived at the house of my friend Yusuf and his wife, Nasrin, they greeted us with immense relief . . . and with food. In Bangladeshi culture, you accept food when it's offered to you, no matter the hour. It'd be rude to say no, as your hosts expect you to eat something. It's how we show our guests that we care for them.

After eating, I slept for a few hours. Then we all set off for Auckland Airport to welcome Husna, the dream lady who was going to be my wife forever. In the hours before her arrival, my nerves about our marriage had completely dissipated, only to be replaced by an overwhelming concern for Husna's well-being. It was such a long trip—she had begun on a train from Sylhet to Dhaka with some of her family, then she'd boarded a plane for Singapore, then another for Auckland. All up, it took more than two days. I was worried about whether she'd eaten on the plane, whether she'd been comfortable, whether she was OK. I was terrified that something might have happened to her. My mind was in overdrive, causing me to feel dizzy and unstable. As a soccer player, I'd frequently abused my poor head by butting the ball, but even so I'd never felt vertigo like this before. I could barely stand up straight. Yusuf noticed my wobbliness and implored me to be strong.

Waiting at the airport, I couldn't stay in one spot for more than a few seconds, and eventually my anxiety propelled me to the airline counter.

'I need details on a particular passenger, please,' I told them.

'I'm sorry, sir,' the attendant said. 'Our privacy policy prohibits the release of personal details without identification.'

The creases in my worried face deepened and, seeing my desperation, the attendant softened.

'What was the name? OK, yes, I can confirm that she is indeed aboard.'

That granted me a little relief, but not for long.

Soon, Husna appeared in the arrivals hall. She looked exhausted and thin. Clearly unwell, but still smiling, she leaned heavily on the shoulder of the lady escorting her. When she saw me, her smile broadened and her eyes filled with tears.

My own eyes welled up in response.

In unison, in our hearts, we thanked Allah Almighty for His mercy. Husna was here, at long last.

Now we just had to get married.

BEFORE WE COULD EVEN CONSIDER officialising our marriage, however, we had to first make it out to the car. As I looked at my weak bride-to-be, I was faced with a new dilemma. It was clear that she wouldn't be able to walk to the car without help, but since we weren't yet husband and wife I was not allowed to touch her. At the same time, I was her family now, the person who would take care of her and be—as her strange dream had foreseen—both her husband and her father. So, silently asking God to forgive me, I bundled her up in my arms.

She was light as a feather. It transpired that she had not been able to eat a thing in the days leading up to her long journey. She couldn't work out why she had lost her appetite, but I understood: it was the result of her worry. The bold act of coming all this way on her own had demanded a high price, and now she was so weak she could barely walk. The realisation of how much it had cost her, emotionally and physically, to come here brought the tears back to my eyes.

Once we got to the car, and Husna was safely inside, it was time to turn my attention to the next task for the day: our wedding. Fortunately for me, upon returning to Yusuf and Nasrin's home, I discovered my friends had already taken care of the venue, the food and the decorating: their place was full of colour, people and the aroma of a delicious feast. It was all so beautiful and meticulous that I realised they must have been planning it for weeks. Husna and I never forgot the kindness and thoughtfulness our friends showed us on our wedding day.

All that was left for me to do was to find a Muslim celebrant to conduct the ceremony. I hadn't organised one ahead of time, since I'd assumed I'd find someone easily enough—I had lived in Auckland for four years when I first arrived in New Zealand, and during that time I had given talks at local mosques, so I knew a few imams.

Yusuf came with me to a nearby mosque. The imam already knew me well, but even so he refused to solemnise my marriage to Husna.

'She has no guardian present,' he stated. 'I will not marry her without permission from her guardian.'

'But she *does* have permission from her guardian,' I tried to explain. 'They permitted her to come here so that she could marry me. I need to fulfil my promise to marry her.'

But the imam would not budge. He was not a tough nut to crack; he was uncrackable.

I wholeheartedly respected his position, and I also felt ashamed: I had brought my bride all this way, asked her to take a leap of faith, and here I was letting her down, all because I hadn't done my homework properly. I was so disappointed in myself. All I could think of was Husna, waiting for me back at my friends' house, trusting that I would be sorting everything out. I had to do something—but what?

I sat there in the mosque, racking my brains. I knew we could simply go to a registry office and marry legally without a celebrant, but I wanted us to have the blessing of a Muslim cleric. Then a name came to my mind: Sheikh Muhammad Khalil. He was an imam and a Muslim scholar I knew, and for some reason I felt as though I should call him. So I did.

He listened calmly as I explained my predicament, and when he replied I could hear the smile in his voice.

'Come to my place, Brother Farid,' he said. 'Let's discuss it together.'

Yusuf and I didn't waste a second. We headed straight there.

When I arrived, Sheikh Khalil was waiting, ready to have afternoon tea. He was in no hurry at all, smiling benignly, and I realised he just wanted to enjoy some time together. But I had no appetite, and I was growing frantic. The pressure I was under drove me straight to the point.

'I am not worried about food right now,' I said. 'I need to get married! Will you solemnise our marriage? I need to know now. Please.'

Sheikh Khalil laughed. 'So eager, Brother Farid! What's the hurry? Can't you wait to get married?'

He was teasing me, and his joke made me blush, but his amicable manner gave me hope. He didn't seem worried about things, and that helped to calm me a little.

'Please, let's eat first,' he insisted. 'We'll talk about your marriage afterwards.'

I relented and ate a few morsels, realising I was actually hungry. As I placed my empty cup of tea back on its saucer, he finally got down to business.

'You name the time and the place, Brother Farid,' he said. 'I will be there for you. I know you are an exemplary Muslim, and I believe your intentions for your wedding are honourable.'

It was turning out to be a day of tears: I was so relieved and grateful that I cried yet again. All the worry and stress that had been building inside me evaporated in an instant. May Allah bless Sheikh Khalil for the kindness he showed us that day.

AS SOON AS WAS POLITE, I raced back to Yusuf and Nasrin's place to ensure that Husna would be ready when Sheikh Khalil arrived to confirm our marriage. But Nasrin was two steps ahead of me. She, along with some other kind-hearted women she knew, had been at home preparing Husna. I returned to find them gathered together, Husna still weak but looking happy.

At last, she and I had a little time alone together, and we talked through our plans. We had already discussed what sort of wedding we wanted, and were both in agreement: simple would be best. This was in line with the teaching of the Prophet Muhammad (peace be upon him) that 'the most blessed wedding is the one done without complication' (Bayhaqi).

The material aspects of the wedding were not what was important to either of us. A happy marriage is not about money or how elaborate the wedding is. A wedding should respect the holy commitment that two people are making to one another, and any ensuing celebration is an opportunity to share happily whatever the couple has. In my time, I have seen some exceptionally extravagant weddings, but they are not as a rule the happiest ones: sometimes, beneath the beautiful exterior, runs a current of stress and anxiety—the opposite of a peaceful union.

'God blesses the simplest of marriages,' Husna said. 'A simple wedding is not only less complicated, but will help us to avoid extravagance or arrogance. There won't be any distraction, and we'll be able to concentrate on what matters: our commitment to and love for one another.'

Even though she was just 20 years old, my young bride had wisdom beyond her age, and she was able to look at our marriage with maturity right from the very start. We both saw a difference between the religious aspects of a wedding and the cultural expectations. The religious requirements were straightforward—we, the bride and groom, simply needed the support of our guardians, two witnesses, a qualified Muslim celebrant, and to promise to take one another in marriage in the name of Allah. I would also give a gift to my new bride, as a token of my responsibility to care for her as her husband. Any expectations beyond this would be cultural ones, and might have led to extravagance and pressure that Husna and I preferred to avoid. We wanted a simple wedding for Allah's blessings.

Keeping things simple would also allow us to save our money, so that we could use it to help other, poorer couples who might not be able to get married without it.

It might sound as though our decision to keep everything simple was an easy one, but that's not quite true. Actually, it was one of the hardest decisions that Husna and I ever made, because what was at stake was our future together. It was a decision that both of us had given a lot of thought to, and it was based not on emotion but on practicality. We received criticism from some relatives and friends who did not understand that, through our simple wedding, we were choosing to practise our religion. Some felt we should have had a big celebration with all the flourishes and fanfare, but over time those who had ridiculed our simple wedding saw that our decision had been the correct one for us. We were so happy together. Husna and I viewed our wedding as an investment in our shared future, something that we needed to carefully manage together so that it would bear fruit for us.

Our simple wedding was the best wedding we could have ever dreamed of. We exchanged our vows with serenity in our hearts, full of the feelings of happiness that Allah wants a newlywed couple to enjoy. We were not worried about fulfilling cultural expectations, or about worldly things. We shared pure joy with one another on that happy day.

The ceremony was over within an hour—the first of many hours that we would spend together as man and wife. From that day forward, Husna and I were part of one another. We had begun with simplicity, and so we carried on. My wife and I celebrated every day that we spent together on this earth as though it were our wedding day.

6.

Determination

দৃঢ় সংকল্প

TWO DAYS AFTER OUR WEDDING, Husna and I packed our things and set off for Nelson. The friend I had picked up in Hastings came with us. I had thought that we would be able to treat the trip home as something of a sightseeing excursion to welcome Husna to her new country. However, I'd underestimated just how taxing the voyage from Bangladesh would be, and the additional stress that such a long road trip would place on my new bride.

Husna was deeply uncomfortable for the entire trip from Auckland down to Wellington. She was plagued with dizziness, headaches and cramps. It was fortunate my friend was there to drive, as I spent the time sitting in the back seat with Husna, doing everything I could think of to try to ease the journey for her.

I massaged her head and legs, opened the window to allow fresh air into the car, closed the window to stop the wind, and let her rest her head on my shoulder when she needed to. I sang, talked, told jokes. We stopped often so that Husna could get out and walk around, leaning on me. Sometimes I had to carry her. I was very concerned about her. I knew she was not enjoying the trip, and as a result I wasn't enjoying it either. Seeing how unwell she was, my friend decided he would help us by driving all the way back to Nelson.

When we got to Wellington, we boarded the ferry bound for Picton, and at long last I saw Husna relax. She spent those few hours as we crossed Cook Strait watching the ocean. Many people feel seasick on boats, but not Husna. She watched the waves silently, pensively, and it was as though she were taking solace from the sea. Human emotion is not dissimilar to an ocean, with its pitching, rolling waves. As I watched Husna, I could almost see her diving beneath the waves roiling inside her, down to the bottom of whatever it was that she was feeling. I wanted to know what she was thinking, but I dared not disrupt her meditation.

When we got to Picton, however, it was back into the car for another few hours for the drive to Nelson, and Husna's discomfort immediately returned. Where she had been completely at ease with the ferry cresting and dipping as it rode the waves, the swinging motion of the car twisting and turning along the winding road to Nelson made her nauseous. She threw up more than once during the drive, and on me, since I was still sitting with her. I'd never had someone be sick on me before, and it's something I would normally have found extremely unpleasant. (I'm a caring person, but I am still human, after all!) However, something vital had changed in me. The only thing I cared about was Husna. Clothes can be washed, while I already felt that Husna was a part of me. Her discomfort was my own. Later, after our daughter was born, I felt exactly the same way about our little baby.

Around 9.30 p.m., we finally arrived at my home in Nelson, and I put Husna to bed, hoping to give her some rest. As I was leaving the bedroom to go and prepare some food for us, she spoke up.

'Please, don't go,' she said. 'Stay with me.'

Her breathing had changed. It was coming in short, shallow gasps.

'I can't breathe,' she said. 'I think I'm going to die.'

She looked terrified, and a cold feeling washed over me.

'I'm going to take you to the hospital,' I said.

'No, no. Please, just stay here with me. I don't want to die alone.'

My mind was full of prayers to Allah, begging for his help. I did not know what to do, and inside I felt as afraid as Husna looked. Worst-case scenarios began to hurtle through my imagination like a tornado, tearing up any calm or peace that might have been there and strewing panic in its wake. But I did not show my distress to Husna. Instead, I surrendered to Allah's mercy. I drowned out my fears by praying aloud to him, speaking clearly so that Husna would hear me and be able to join in. I sat on the bed and put her head in my lap.

'I am here with you,' I said to Husna between my prayers. 'You are not alone. You need not worry.'

I repeated these words and my prayers over and over, and after about five minutes Husna's breathing began to return to normal.

She looked up at me and she smiled, and I felt my own racing heart start to slow with relief.

'I think I am OK now,' she said. 'I feel much better.'

I was so relieved. Together, we thanked Allah profusely.

Then I said, 'We still need to eat. Come with me.'

Although Husna's distress had abated, I did not want to leave her on her own, so I carried her to the sofa. I had thought she could rest there while I made our food, but she was having none of it.

'Here, let me help you with that,' she said, getting up from the couch.

'No, you need to rest,' I said. 'Stay there. I can do it.'

'I can't sit here and watch while you're working! I must do something.'

Husna would not take no for an answer. We finally ate at around midnight. As I would discover, my wife was stubborn when it came to caring for others—and when it came to many other things, too. No matter what Husna's own condition was, she would always insist upon helping in whatever way she could. She was like that every day of her life.

THERE WERE MANY THINGS THAT Husna had to learn when she arrived in New Zealand, and cooking was one of them. Many young people in Bangladesh are so busy with their studies that they do not have time to cook; other family members do the cooking, or a family might hire someone to do it for them. Husna had no idea how to cook. Teaching her was one of my first jobs as her husband.

'We're going to start with a cup of tea,' I told her.

'Too easy!' she said.

'It's best to begin with the basics,' I replied. 'And, since you already know how to do it, you can show me. Please, make a cup of tea for each of us.'

Husna didn't waste any time and soon appeared bearing two cups of tea.

'Here you go!' she said proudly.

'You taste it first,' I said. 'I'd like you to tell me what you think. Then I'll taste it and give you my feedback.'

Husna beamed confidently at me as she raised her cup and took a sip—then suddenly spat the tea back into the cup. I was already lifting my own cup, but paused, my hand frozen halfway through the motion.

'Stop! Don't drink it!' she said. 'It's horrible! I put salt in it instead of sugar!'

She burst out laughing, and I did too. We laughed for a long time about that. Husna learned her first lesson well: a cook must always try their food to check it tastes OK before they serve it to others.

AS WELL AS COOKING, HUSNA also had to learn how to speak English. She found this much more difficult. Mastering a language is never easy, and doing so takes a clever person a lot of hard work. Husna was both smart and diligent, and she put those skills to good use learning her new language.

Again, I was her teacher. Back in Bangladesh, I had volunteered as an English teacher at a high school. Then I'd learned how to speak the language here in New Zealand; I'd already been here five years when Husna joined me. It's not uncommon for one spouse to teach another in this way, but it can be a fraught process. For example, sometimes the teacher can't resist telling the student off for their mistakes—and mistakes are many when you're learning to speak a new language. What begins with the best of intentions can end with husband and wife arguing or refusing to talk to one another, and any learning falls by the wayside.

Fortunately, Husna and I never faced this problem. It probably helped that we are both hard workers with caring natures. We learned how important it is to be patient, gentle and respectful towards your spouse whenever they're learning something new—whether it's a language or anything else.

Before long, Husna's warm smile had won her numerous offers of free lessons from new friends, and she'd soon picked up more than the basics. Within six months, she was able to communicate effectively in her new language, and her accent when speaking English eventually became less noticeable than mine. Her hard work paid off.

Husna believed in learning as a responsibility. To not learn, to not make the effort to pick up new things, was in her mind a crime. As a recent arrival to New Zealand, Husna felt she owed it to the country that had opened its arms to her to work hard. Focusing on learning English well and as quickly as possible was one way for her to show her appreciation. Speaking English would allow her to become a fully participating Kiwi, someone who contributed to the wider community in her new home. It would allow her to give back to the country that had given to her.

Her inspiration for this philosophy lay in the story in the Quran of the prophet Joseph (peace be upon him). Joseph first arrived in Egypt as a young man, having been bought as a slave by a rich man and then welcomed into the man's home. Joseph worked very hard out of a sense of duty and thanks towards his new country, and he became a great contributor to Egypt. His admirable work ethic won the hearts of so many. I share Husna's belief. Just like she did, I feel I owe New Zealand so much for having welcomed me when I immigrated here. It's my duty to give back as much as I can, just as Joseph did for Egypt.

Holding true to her philosophy, Husna also wanted to get a job as soon as she could. As my wife, she was not required to work; it is my duty, as a Muslim man, to provide for my wife. But Husna *wanted* to work—she wanted to contribute financially to our home and to her new country, and she didn't much like staying at home on her own while I was out at work.

Getting a job was not a straightforward matter for her, though. First, she had to wait six months before she got a work visa. Then, she struggled because of her initial lack of both English and relevant job skills. She was also unsure of how potential employers might feel about her wearing her headscarf.

Husna did not let these issues hold her back. I could see that she was determined to get a job, so I did what I could to help, and eventually I persuaded a salmon-processing plant to give her a trial. When they immediately hired her for the remainder of the season, I was not at all surprised. Who wouldn't want someone who was such a quick learner, so hard-working and with such a friendly smile on their team?

After that job, Husna soon found a permanent position as a machinist at Independent Casing Co. Ltd. Not only did she enjoy working hard, but she loved spending time with her colleagues, making friends and learning about New Zealand culture. She worked with a group of ladies who were very kind and made her feel completely at home. Soon, she was inviting people round to eat at our house. Husna loved feeding people as much as I do. Welcoming people from all walks of life into our home has always given us the opportunity to learn from those with different mindsets and backgrounds from our own.

Husna was never afraid of a challenge. At one point, she set her sights on a job shucking scallops at a local seafood factory. She'd heard it paid well—the more you shucked, the more you earned— and it would also give her the chance to learn another new skill. However, she had no relevant experience, so the company's manager was naturally reluctant to take her on. 'I'm sorry,' he said when she and I went to talk to him. 'We don't have any work here that's suitable for you.'

My persistent wife was not going to let him off the hook that easily. She quickly listed all of the reasons he should give her a chance. 'Just give me a three-day trial,' she said. 'Then you'll see what a good employee I am.'

I saw a look of annoyance cross his face, but it was mixed with surprise at the determination of this woman before him. He called in the floor supervisor.

'Let's give her a go,' she said, once she'd heard Husna's case. 'A trial can't hurt.'

So Husna trotted off to work the next day and came home with a job for the rest of the season. In no time, she became one of their most experienced and valuable team members, and had accrued a whole new collection of ladies as her friends. Husna's smile really was magical: it melted the reserve of even the surliest strangers so that, before they knew it, they'd become her friend.

WHEN SHE'D BEEN IN NEW ZEALAND three years, Husna decided it was time to start working for herself. She'd learned a lot working for others, but she was ready for a change. Being self-employed would give her more flexibility and be better suited to her personality and her values. I felt my wife was being overly ambitious, but I also knew her very well. I knew that 'ambitious' was just part of who she was, and that she would not give up on the idea without trying first.

So I helped Husna set up a takeaway shop called Indian Food in a Nelson mall. She knew what a huge challenge running her own business would be, but she didn't shy away from it. If anything, that only made the opportunity all the more attractive to her. She wanted to test herself out, to see if she was capable of it—and she was. Her business did well, and she enjoyed every day of it. It demanded an enormous amount of work from her, but she embraced it true to form: she cooked and cleaned, charmed her customers, and ran a tight ship to reduce her costs and maximise her profits.

The experience of running her own business gave Husna so much more than money. It consolidated her already excellent leadership skills by improving her confidence and resilience, and further reinforced to her the merits of hard work.

THERE WAS ONE MORE THING Husna wanted to learn when she arrived in New Zealand, and that was how to drive a car. Kiwis take a lot of delight in doing things for themselves, and their cars are no different—they drive them, clean them, fill them with petrol, change their tyres, tinker with them and in some cases modify them in strange and creative ways. A car is often more than a vehicle; it becomes a means of self-sufficiency. When Husna saw the way that men and women alike drive themselves about here, she couldn't wait to have a go at it herself.

So she got herself a learner's licence, passing the test with flying colours. Then she got in the car with her driving instructor—me. Teaching your spouse to drive a car can go a similar route to trying to teach them another language, if you're not careful. Out of love, it can be easy to be overprotective and cautious, yelling when the learner driver makes mistakes. We all know how that story can end. So, just as I did with cooking, I started with the basics. Slowly, Husna's confidence behind the wheel grew.

Then, one day while I was working in my study, Husna appeared. She looked worried.

'What's wrong?' I asked. 'Did something happen?'

'I don't want to drive anymore,' she said firmly.

I realised something significant must have occurred. It took a lot to make my wife give up on one of her quests just like that.

'OK,' I said gently, not wanting to pressure her, but also wondering what could have happened. Then I added, as a test to see how she'd respond, 'No more driving for you, then.'

She was clearly not happy about this, but she was also reluctant to tell me more. Eventually, I managed to extract the details: while she had been out in front of the house practising reversing, she had made a common beginner's error. Instead of pressing the brake, she had jammed her foot down hard on the accelerator. The car had flown forward—and collided with a tree. When I went out to inspect the damage, I saw the front of the car had buckled where it had hit the trunk.

'I think you should give it another go,' I said to Husna. 'I will sit in the car with you.'

'No,' she said.

Husna dug her heels in, but so did I. This time I was not going to concede the victory. I made her realise that, if she didn't at least try again, I would be hurt and disappointed.

My wife faced a dilemma. On the one hand, her confidence had been punctured, but on the other I was making it clear, as her husband, that I wanted to see her try again. Her love for me won out over her fear. She got back into the car.

'We're going to the panelbeaters,' I said. 'You're going to drive us there.'

She did, and when we got there the panelbeater assessed the dent and scratched his chin.

'That's an easy fix,' he said. 'I can have it done in a jiffy. Go out and get yourselves an ice cream, and by the time you come back it'll be ready to drive home.'

We did as we were told, and the panelbeater was true to his word.

And, just as she'd done with speaking English, Husna soon overtook me in the driving stakes, despite that little speed wobble. I'd had to sit my full licence test twice, but Husna passed hers on her first go. I couldn't work out whether it was because I'd been a really good teacher, or because she was a better student than me, but to Husna's credit it was probably the latter. Either way, it didn't matter. Husna was over the moon.

My star student never forgot about the day she drove into the tree.

'Do you remember how you made me get back in the car?' she would say to me. 'You really had to push me to do it.'

She was right—but when she said 'push' what she really meant was 'carry', because that is indeed what I'd been forced to do in order to get my wife back into her car! Husna's persistence could be both a boon and a burden. When she really wanted to achieve something it took the form of tenacity, but when she decided not to do something it could become stubborn refusal. Husna was one determined lady.

7.

Success

সাফল্য

WHAT MARRIAGE DOESN'T FACE ITS trials? Our wedding day was one full of happiness, but also of obstacles, and our life together was no different.

Husna and I soon realised that happiness in marriage is the product of hard work. It does not pour like rain from the sky the moment that two people say 'I do', and it's not a syrup you can pop down to the pharmacy and purchase. In order for a couple to find happiness in their marriage, they need to find a point of unity and to respect one another. Otherwise, happiness remains out of reach, little more than a fantasy, a relic of the fairy tales we read when we're young, in which everyone lives happily ever after.

Right from the beginning, Husna and I were clear about what

we wanted for our marriage: to be married forever, in this life and in Paradise. In order to achieve our shared goal, we were willing to make whatever sacrifices we must. Any journey of worth will face its setbacks, and Husna and I both understood this. Our shared wisdom was our secret weapon: whenever we faced difficulties, we struggled and compromised and persevered together. We did what was necessary. We were a team.

Every day we talked to one another about what was going on in our lives, and this bound us together even more tightly. Talking and sharing openly helped us to navigate the bumps in the road, and even in some cases avoid them altogether.

Husna and I shared a positive outlook. We always found a way to see the good in whatever situations we faced. In Islam, loving and caring for your spouse is a good deed, and the more good deeds you do, the better. The teachings of Islam helped us to maintain this positive frame of mind, and encouraged us to continue our hard work without complaint. We saw hardship as a test from God and—always diligent students—we happily struggled to pass every test.

Husna and I were always content and full of hope. Many people who knew us would comment on how our marriage provided an example to others. Young people who were about to get married would say to us, 'I hope that my marriage is as happy as yours.'

Our happiness did not come from our sameness. In fact, it was a product of our differences. We did not always agree, and that was a good thing. It provided an avenue for us to engage our intellects in debate, and to work out together how to go about making the best decision for everyone. We always allowed time to think things over then discuss them before we made any important shared decision. That way, we ensured that we had made the decision together.

AS I HAVE MENTIONED, HUSNA and her family did not place any conditions on me before our wedding. That was not Husna's style. She did not want me to give her anything of material value, as money was not what she got married for.

Nonetheless, I wanted to give my wife a gift of some sort. I wanted to make her happy, and to honour her.

In Auckland, before our wedding, I asked her to tell me what I could give her.

'Your love is the most precious gift to me,' she said. 'I do not want anything else.'

'But I am required by the rule of Islam to give you something,' I persisted. 'There must be something I can give you that will please you.'

But Husna would not budge, would not name a thing that I could give her besides my love. I was learning early just how obstinate my wife could be when it came to her morals. It was hard work to try to convince her to let me give her something of material value—but it was fun, too. I could see that, just as my bride was stubborn in her values, she was also fierce in her love, and that was a great gift to me.

Husna, for her part, was receiving an education in how obstinate her new husband was. I pestered her until she finally conceded.

'You win!' she said at last. 'You can give me one hundred dollars as a wedding gift.'

I grinned—but she hadn't finished.

'I will only keep it for ten minutes,' she added, 'and then I will return it to you.'

I had to surrender to this compromise. I could see that my generous and kind wife would not let money tarnish the purity of her love for me. There was nothing I could say or do that would move her on that. Really, it was Husna who had won, and I let her—for the moment.

OFTEN DURING OUR MARRIED LIFE, I would gift Husna with victory. Many husbands do not realise that letting their wife win is another way of showing love. Our Prophet (peace be upon him) used this technique with his own beloved wife Ayesha (may Allah bestow mercy upon her). One day, the two had a race, and he allowed his wife to win, which resulted in happiness for both: she was happy, so he was too.

This was a tactic I employed many times with Husna, as she liked to win as much as I did. I would let her win, then pretend I hadn't noticed that's what had happened. Probably she realised what I was up to, but either way it was fun to see her glee at her success.

Four days after our wedding, I started a new race with Husna, and this one I intended to win. My mission was to convince her to take—and keep—a gift from me. I put all of my most persuasive skills to work, and we went round and round for a long time.

'Don't try to persuade me,' Husna said. 'I won't change my mind.'

But I kept going, and eventually my reasoning won out.

'You've given so many good reasons that I can't say no now!'

she cried. Then she smiled at me. 'But that's OK.'

At last, I had got her to agree: I would buy her some gold jewellery, and I would also purchase two forestry shares in her name. The shares would take about 30 years to mature—around the time that Husna would turn 50—and would hopefully pay out a good sum of money that she could use however she saw fit. My wife was excited about that idea, thinking of all the good ways she could put her gift to use for others.

MY BRIDE MIGHT NOT HAVE wanted to take a gift from me, but she did have expectations. She had been quite clear to herself about what she wanted in a groom, and had an intimidating list of standards for me to meet. So did I fulfil her criteria? I cannot answer that, of course. All I can say is that I know Husna was happy with me, and I am happy with that. I do not think myself perfect, but I found Husna to be perfect in every quality she had hoped to find in me. She had high expectations for her husband because she had high expectations of herself. She wanted her husband to always be striving in the same way that she was.

Over time, I came to learn precisely how Husna's dream of me as both her husband and her father had guided her into our marriage. It told her that she needed me to love and care for her not only as her spouse, but also as a parent. This was no small expectation. It placed an enormous responsibility upon my shoulders, in the form of her total trust in me. I accepted it completely and without complaint, but the sheer weight of it also terrified me. I did not want to let her down. The love between a couple is very different from that between a parent and child. Sometimes couples separate, but the parent–child bond is forever. A husband and wife might love one another conditionally, but a parent loves their child unconditionally. Spouses can be careless and irresponsible with one another, but it is a parent's responsibility to keep their child safe. If a husband makes a mistake, his wife won't necessarily provide comfort; by comparison, if a child commits an error, they should be able to run, crying, to their parent for guidance. When I accepted this dual responsibility, it was my turn to be brave. I promised myself I would never break Husna's heart.

Sometimes, Husna's high expectations and her intense care for others could manifest as frustration if she ever found herself disappointed. She was a perfectionist, always trying to do her very best, and she expected no less from her loved ones. When it came to being her husband, that meant she would sometimes get angry with me if she ever felt I wasn't meeting her commitment head on. She had invested a hundred per cent of her love and trust in me, and if she perceived anything less on my side she would feel neglected and let down. Her anger never lasted for long, though.

I could tell when she was upset with me, because she'd become a bit grumpy and uncharacteristically silent. It was commonly one of a short list of oversights on my part that would cause my wife to be curt with me—if I wasn't punctual, or hadn't cleaned up after myself, or was a bit sloppy in my dress. Whenever I realised she was upset with me, I'd show my sincere love for her, and that was always enough to melt her anger. She was such a caring person that she could never stay mad for long; it went against her gentle nature. Her short-lived frustration was always a reminder to me that goodness is a constant work in progress. There was, and is, always more that every one of us can do to be better.

Once, after we had been married for many years, I went out to mosque for my evening prayer during Ramadan. Husna stayed at home with our daughter, and she made me promise to come home as soon as I was done. She always worried about me going out after dark on my own, and fretted that something might happen to me. Unfortunately, I got caught in an important meeting, and since I didn't have a mobile phone I couldn't call Husna to let her know I'd be late.

Well, Husna started to worry, and her worries grew and grew until they had eclipsed everything else. First, she called some friends to ask if they'd seen me. They said they were pretty sure I'd already left to go home. So Husna called the police. It was only once they were on their way that Husna saw my car pull up outside our house. In that moment, all of her fears for me became anger. She was never an aggressive person, and she loved me too much to ever scold me, but that evening she wanted me to know how upset she was. What could she do?

My loving wife decided she'd lock the door so that I wouldn't be able to get inside, and would instead have to wait for her to open it. Hopefully, while I sat outside in the cold and dark, I would feel bad about disappointing her. She hid behind the door and waited to see what I would do.

I simply unlocked the door from the outside.

I had won that race—or had I?

My gentle wife had chosen the gentlest form of punishment for me, and even though it had backfired on her it still taught me a lesson. She had not yelled at me. She could have been aggressive, could have blamed me for causing her so much worry, but instead she'd shown her disappointment through a calm and careful gesture. As I opened the door, I found her waiting quietly for me, a look of surprise on her face.

I could not speak. I was filled with shame, remorseful for having caused my wife so much concern. When Husna saw the look on my face, she immediately read my feelings.

Bursting into tears, she ran to me and hugged me. 'Never do that to me again!' she said. 'I was so worried about you.'

Husna's love for me was so total, so complete, that it could be overwhelming. I saw the love that hid inside her worry, and I appreciated it as she appreciated my care for her. Our love for one another brought us joy in this life, and we both believed it would bring us the same in Paradise. Thanks to Husna, I know the true value of love as a goldsmith knows gold. It is rare, precious, a gift.

8.

Acceptance

গ্রহণযোগ্যতা

THE DAY THAT I WAS hit by a drunk driver in a speeding car, our lives took a U-turn. Up until that point, Husna and I had been doing well for ourselves: we both had good jobs and decent incomes, and we enjoyed sharing our good fortune with others. We hosted many people at our home each week, but we were also careful with our money and saved some of it. The future looked bright.

That awful accident changed everything. Suddenly we both became jobless. I couldn't work, for obvious reasons—first I had to learn how to live with my significantly altered circumstances— and Husna couldn't work because she had to care for me. No jobs meant no money, but Husna didn't give that any thought in the immediate aftermath.

Her sole focus was on me, and on helping me to get better.

When I awoke from my coma and started talking again, our financial circumstances caused me great concern, and I spoke about this with my wife. When I had made my holy marriage vows, I had committed to taking responsibility for Husna's financial security. But how was I supposed to be her provider when I couldn't work? How was I supposed to take care of her when it had suddenly become her job to care for me? I was very worried.

Husna came to my rescue. 'We shall live within our means,' she said. 'Do not worry about it, *priyō*. We will find a way.'

I knew that I needed to simply do my best, then put my trust in Allah, but I was so shattered after my accident—in every way imaginable—that I struggled to calm my worries. Husna's support was crucial to me in those trying weeks and months. She constantly reminded me that we were a team. '*Amora jotoi badhar sommukhin hoina keno, amora akothrey mukabela korbo*,' she would say. *No matter what comes our way, we will face it together.*

It was in those darkest of days that the brightness and purity of Husna's love shone clear to me. She showed me what true love looks like: it is a love that keeps a person alongside their spouse for better and worse, a love that turns negativity into positivity. My wife held my hand and stood by me when I needed it most. She was an inspiration to me, an example of what marriage is all about.

So together, as Husna had said, we rebuilt our lives to accommodate the ways in which our world had changed. Initially, Husna raised the possibility of her returning to work to support the both of us, but that was one thing I could not bring myself to accept. I was already acutely aware of how diminished my role as

Husna's provider had become as a result of the accident, and my heart just could not bear the idea of her being forced to provide for me financially as well, on top of everything she was already doing. I received a small amount of money from ACC (Accident Compensation Corporation) and, for a while, from Work and Income, and we could manage with what we had if we were careful.

We decided we would live more frugally, and accept what we had without complaint. It was another test for us, and we would rise to meet it with grace and with hope. We became thriftier in every way that we could, cooking at home and growing our own vegetables, buying our clothes more cheaply, and not taking holidays. There is no way that we could have done all of this if Husna had not been by my side in the endeavour. She embraced our new circumstances wholeheartedly, and persevered by doing everything she could to make our lives comfortable within our limited means.

Out of the restricting of our financial situation came something surprising: our spiritual freedom expanded. When we made the decision to live within our meagre means, we didn't realise that we were liberating ourselves from financial anxieties that might have otherwise burdened us. Our simple lifestyle proved to hold the same precious lessons as our simple wedding had. Money doesn't necessarily lead to happiness. We learned to be happy with what we had, and discovered that true richness of the heart lies in being free from material desires. We might have found ourselves with less money, but we ended up with more time for others and for each other. Our already strong bond became invincible, and we found a new level of happiness in our marriage. What had begun as a story of loss transformed into a lesson on enrichment.

OF COURSE, IT WASN'T JUST our financial situation that changed following my accident. Our whole lives changed, and with them our roles towards one another as husband and wife.

Before the accident, I had been Husna's teacher, showing her how to drive, how to speak English, how to set up and run her own business. It was me who changed the lightbulbs in our house, who did the gardening and mowed the lawn, who painted the deck and kept our house shipshape. That drunk driver, through his reckless actions, didn't just steal my ability to walk; he also took away so many other things I had previously done for my wife. But Husna inherited those tasks from me without complaint and with her famous smile on her face. As always, she took the challenge in her stride, learning and growing before my eyes, and motivating me to do the same.

Accepting that her husband would be wheelchair-bound for the rest of his life was a challenge unlike any other Husna had yet faced. Many women from my culture would break down if something similar happened to them. They'd be frightened about doing things for themselves, about having to manage independently, and wouldn't be brave enough to do everything on their own—but Husna was exceptional. She was brave. Many people struggle against accepting the things that happen to them, and in the process cause themselves misery, but Husna was not one of those people. She accepted her fate without question, without hesitation, and doing so gave her total peace of mind. Her deep faith freed her from wishing that things were different, and instead she thanked Allah for the gifts that He had given her.

This capacity to accept and be thankful enabled Husna to

respond to even the most tragic of circumstances with positivity. Some relatives back home did not hesitate to tell her what they thought of her husband being in a wheelchair. They made cruel, unkind comments. They were critical and negative. But Husna's smile acted like a torch. When people came to her complaining or criticising, she shone the light of her own calmness and wisdom on their poor behaviour. In doing so, she gently guided them to see their negative actions for what they truly were.

Husna was happy with what she had, and she wasn't worried about what others thought. She drew on her faith and let it show her how to adjust her life around my disability, and she did so with grace and care. There is the saying that a friend in need is a friend indeed, and Husna was my best friend, a friend who loved me truly. Husna knew that my independent nature inhibited me from asking for help, so she never waited for me to ask. She was simply there, ready to provide assistance the moment it was needed, in order to save me from having to request it.

In her care for me, she could sometimes become bossy, telling me off if I did something that would put my health at risk. We were a pair! She wouldn't rest when I told her she needed to, and if the roles were reversed the dynamic remained exactly the same.

I greatly appreciated my wife's care for me. Through it, she showed me her love and respect. No matter how busy she was, Husna always maintained a sense of humour, telling jokes and making me smile.

WHILE HUSNA ACCEPTED OUR NEW life with grace and positivity, I found it more difficult to adjust. Before the accident,

I had walked and run about every day, but that ability had been taken from me in one swift and horrifying hit.

Like Husna, I never held a grudge against the driver—he had made a terrible mistake, and he never apologised for it, but that was not something I had to hold on to. Instead, I did as Husna did and forgave him, completely and unconditionally. Life is short, and I want to do as much good while I am here as possible. Holding on to hate and resentment poisons the will to do good; it contaminates a person's peace of mind and only holds them back from doing good deeds. I had been made a victim by that man's thoughtless actions, but I refused to become a victim of anger and hatred as well.

Forgiving the driver was easy; it was accepting the direct impact his actions had on me that was challenging. 'How am I going to live like this?' I asked myself. I struggled to see how I could carry on living a good life when I was stuck in a wheelchair. In my eyes, I was utterly dependent, completely useless. My body and my soul were in agony, and I felt hope slipping away from me. I didn't know how to carry on.

Those were very painful days. My faith does not permit a person to take their own life, so that was never something I considered, but I did pray to Allah for a peaceful death. In the depths of that disaster, I was having trouble seeing how I could make my way forward into the future.

My attentive wife soon caught on to what I was praying for.

'Dua koro valor jonno,' she told me. *Pray for better.*

Husna's positivity did for me what it did for so many others during her time here on earth: it showed me that there was another way, a brighter way, and that beyond the shadows lay hope. I just had to adjust my gaze.

9.
Generosity

দাক্ষিণ্য

AFTER I'D BEEN IN BURWOOD Hospital in Christchurch for six months, Husna and I were finally able to return to Nelson. Our friends there were an amazing support, and we settled back in to our home. However, four months later, I had to go back to Burwood for an assessment. Travelling there was so trying that Husna and I decided it would be best to move to Christchurch permanently, so we could be closer to the doctors and rehabilitation specialists. I was very emotional about leaving Nelson. While I sobbed, Husna comforted me and reassured me that we would do it together, that it would be OK.

In November 1998, we officially made Christchurch our home, and we have been here ever since. There are people here from all walks of life, and the city's recent hardships have exposed the remarkable resilience and compassion of its residents. I feel that this special city loves me, and I love her too. It's a little like a parent–child relationship, this love I have for my city and her people: despite our ups and downs, I love Christchurch no matter what, and with every peak and trough that love deepens. My daughter was born here. This flat city welcomed me in my wheelchair. I came here for my recovery, and both I and my wife were cared for and embraced by so many kind people here. Our family has made our home here, and we are part of the fabric of this place. We will always be grateful for the kindness and love we have received here, and we feel we owe the city the same in return.

When we arrived in Christchurch, Husna and I found ourselves at a crossroads. My accident had forced an overhaul of our day-to-day life, and in the process encouraged us to really think about the direction we wanted our future together to take. We talked about it a lot, as we always did about every important shared decision. We agreed that we wanted to do what made us both happiest—but happy in a spiritual sense, not a material one. It could not be just anything; it had to be something meaningful, rewarding, holy. In accordance with the teachings of Islam, Husna and I both believe that, when you receive help, you should try to give something back.

My wife listened to her heart, and it told her the same thing it had told her since she was a child: to give, freely and without expectation of recompense. Husna's independence took a very similar form to my own—she was always keen to give, and found it difficult to receive. When we decided that Husna should not work after my accident, and that we would live simply off what we had, that opened the door to my wife's dreams. It gave her the freedom to do the things she always loved the most: giving to and helping others.

We were on the same page. I was so happy to hear that she wanted to dedicate her time, energy and talents to unpaid work. It was a choice that complemented my own aspirations, and I promised I would do everything within my power to support her. I was always very supportive of Husna and her dreams, as she was of me and mine. That was how we worked together.

So we made up our minds to focus on serving our fellow humans, free of charge. We would make ends meet with the little income I earned from ACC and from my homeopathy practice, and we would dedicate our time to benefiting others as much as we could.

DONATING HER TIME AND TALENTS for the good of others was in Husna's blood, and was a happy match with her charming personality. The hardships she had experienced in her own life had taught her how to empathise, and how to listen. It can be difficult for a person to understand how to be truly kind if they haven't suffered themselves. Husna transformed the cruelties she'd faced into love, and her kind nature gave her the ability to provide comfort to others. The grief she had experienced in her own life taught her about pain, and made her passionate about doing what she could to relieve the pain of others.

Neither Husna nor I have ever had a lot of money, but my wife was rich in her heart. She was happy with what we had, and she always shared that good fortune. Material luxury was never something she cared about. Her shopping list was a short one, based on needs and how she could best distribute the little she had to help the most people. 'If everyone in this world shared what they have,' Husna would say, 'nobody would be hungry.' She would make our modest income stretch so that we could contribute to the cost of surgery for sick women in Bangladesh, or to sponsor poor students, or to help out families who weren't well off.

Husna's sense of duty to give and share stemmed from her faith. She believed it was her obligation to do so for the sake of God, and that if she gave without expectation she would earn a place in Paradise. She truly loved helping others, and gave without limits or criteria. She would help anyone, no matter where they came from, or what language they spoke, or what religion they practised.

Husna opened the doors of our home to one and all, and it was a hive of activity. People were always arriving to ask for advice, to share grief and joy, to eat with us, to organise fundraising, to learn, to get a ride somewhere. Often, those same people also appeared to take Husna to her own medical appointments, or to offer their own kindnesses in return. My wife gave her life's work to others, and she filled our house with the most expansive love possible. She was, in the truest sense, a philanthropist, even if she wasn't a wealthy one. In her every action and deed, she sought to promote the welfare of others, and donated the money she had to good causes.

IN NELSON, WE HAD TAUGHT a small class of children about the basics of Islam, and at the suggestion of some local elders we decided to continue doing so in Christchurch. We committed to taking a free class every Sunday at Masjid al-Noor, donating our weekends to the children, to our future generations. When others were taking a break from their weekday jobs, we were happy to sacrifice our time because we believed it was good work. Through our lessons, we hoped to teach children how to become kind, caring Kiwi citizens—it was our gift to New Zealand, just one way that we could give back to the country that had shown us so much love. By teaching children the peaceful values of Islam, we wanted to show them that humanity is one large family, and that we can co-exist in harmony just like the flowers that colour the gardens of our city.

On our very first day taking our class at Masjid al-Noor, 56 children came along—many more than we'd had back in Nelson. As in every other aspect of our life together, Husna and I worked seamlessly as a team: Husna brought her charismatic personality to bear managing the children, while I delivered the teachings. We taught children how to memorise and recite from the Holy Quran in Arabic, and about the five pillars of Islam. We also taught them about Islamic etiquette and values, the stories of the holy prophets (peace be upon them all), and the teachings of the Quran and Hadith, so that they might learn how to be peace-loving people with the best moral character. Husna was both stern and caring as a teacher, and her students loved her. It was always clear that the children felt safe in her company.

Husna also ran lessons at the mosque to teach women how to perform the wrapping of a Muslim sister after death. Washing and wrapping a deceased person's body is an essential part of Muslim funeral rites, and should occur as soon as possible after death. In Islam, cleanliness is an important part of the faith—as well as normal cleaning, Islam teaches us to clean ourselves in a prescribed way that was revealed by Allah to the Prophet (peace be upon him). This teaches us to achieve physical as well as spiritual cleanliness. Allah is pure, as are His angels who accompany the deceased, and He likes His servants to proceed to the next life with purity. Washing the bodies of the dead is therefore very significant in Islam.

There is a particular way to wash and wrap a body, and Husna trained women how to perform this task. She'd carefully take them through each of the steps, including how to cut the shroud so that it would be ready for wrapping the body immediately after washing. She often used a doll to demonstrate. Sometimes, to lighten the mood, she'd then get women to practise on one another. Washing and wrapping is an act of love and respect, and just another way my wife shared with others.

PHILANTHROPY IS ABOUT MORE THAN donating money. It is not only money that people need, and Husna and I both believe that there are more important things a person can give: time, skills, knowledge, advice, ideas and so on. Husna and I wanted to give, and to do so genuinely, so we did not charge for the services we could provide. This required sacrifice on our part, but it was one we were happy to make. In two decades, we did not take any holidays together. Once, Husna took a month-long trip to Bangladesh, but that was it. We spent almost every weekday helping others, and our weekends teaching the young to be peaceful, modest, good Muslim citizens.

Husna was frugal, but her charitable work still required some money. She often used the car, and needed money for petrol, as well as for other things. In order to continue her good work, she needed a weekly fund, so that was what we established. Every week, I made a small deposit into her personal account, and that gave her the freedom to carry on with her work in whatever way she needed to. She could have spent some of that money on herself, but she never did. She put every cent towards the well-being of others. There was always someone whose troubles she felt she could ease with what little she had.

I wanted Husna to have as much as possible, because I felt fortunate to have such a generous wife. The money she spent on her charity work—a good deed—would reap spiritual rewards for both of us.

After my accident, Husna took over managing all of my bank cards. If she'd been a different woman, she might have spent money on her own desires, but she never did that. As generous as she was in giving her money to others, my wife was tight-fisted when it came to herself. Shifa and I would sometimes tease her by calling her stingy, but Husna knew we meant it kindly. I have never met a person as selfless as my wife. She was a rare example of true generosity.

Husna's approach to money was wise. When you die, you can't take money with you. Even so, too many of us spend our lives chasing after that mortal commodity. We desperately grasp at it, holding tight to what we have and avoiding sharing it. When we treat money this way, it doesn't make anyone happy—not us, and certainly not others. We forget that Allah is testing us with money. Will we be generous? Or will we be selfish?

We will only attain true happiness, and a peaceful world, when we learn that we must share with one another. As Husna said, if we all shared freely what we have, there would be no more hunger, no more sick people suffering without treatment, no one going without education or clothing or a roof over their head. Our salvation lies in our capacity to share graciously and wholeheartedly, yet most of us do the opposite and it only causes us all to suffer.

Husna was a smart person. She knew she could not take any money with her to the next life, so while she was here she used what she had to make as many people as she could smile. Even after death, she was donating what she had, bequeathing any money she had to charity. And those forestry shares she let me purchase in her name when we were married? They won't mature for another few years, meaning Husna never lived long enough to receive the wedding gift I wanted to give her. The task of working out what to do with those shares fell to me, and to our daughter, and after some discussion we decided to put them towards wedding gifts for those in need. That's what Husna would have wanted.

Through her generosity, my wife experienced the greatest happiness, which comes from making others happy. May Allah bless her for her generosity. With it, she made the world a better place.

10.
Empathy
সহানুভূতি

CARING FOR OTHERS IS NOT always easy. It requires self-sacrifice. Husna was like a candle, sharing her light with others, but at her own expense. She gave and gave and gave, and she refused to take a break from her good work. The burden was not just physical; it was also emotional. Her family needed her. Her friends needed her. Her community needed her. In a collection of notebooks, she kept lists of the various things she had to do for those she supported and worked with. Her phones rang every day, at all hours, and she would race off to attend to this person or that one. Everyone needed Husna, and she would never say no to those in need.

When you care for others, their worries become yours, and that was certainly true for Husna. Whenever she would head out to help someone, she'd have to leave me alone at home—and she'd end up worrying about me as well as the person she was attending to. She couldn't be in two places at once, but I'm sure that, if she could have, she would have found a way to do just that.

My accident, unsurprisingly, only heightened Husna's worry for me. She had always been concerned about my well-being, because that was who she was, but after my accident the worry began to consume her. She became very protective of me, fretting about my safety, my health, whether I was eating enough. I am not a worrier in the way that Husna was, but even my calmness failed to rub off on her. Once she'd started off down that road, it was hard to get her to turn back. 'Do not worry about me,' I would tell her, but it was never to any avail. It was in her nature to care immensely, and therefore in her nature to worry. Husna's smile provided a handy façade for her to hide her worry behind, so it often went unseen to others, but it was always visible to me.

Husna worried about me and about other people so much that she didn't leave any room for worrying about herself. Eventually, however, her body cried out and made her listen. With increasing frequency and severity, she began experiencing abdominal pain, and she was eventually diagnosed with Crohn's disease, a rare condition that causes inflammation in the digestive tract. Apparently, it is exceptionally uncommon for people from Bangladesh to have Crohn's, but Husna was, as ever, exceptional.

The disease was cruel to my wife. It caused her excruciating pain, and I would feel her agony as though it were my own. I would never wish that sort of suffering on any person, let alone my beloved

Husna. There were times when I would cry helplessly, praying to Allah for her to be cured. Sometimes the disease would throw her into such a critical state that I'd have to rush her to the hospital for immediate relief. I always knew when Husna was in unbearable pain because it was in those moments, and those moments alone, that her smile would slip from her face.

And yet, after each bout, Husna would bounce back as though it were nothing. Mere hours after even the most severe attack, she'd have her smile back on her face and be up and about, cheerfully assisting others and making more new friends in the hospital. She put the past behind her and focused on the moment before her. She did not want to dwell on her pain, but preferred to return to joy as soon as she was physically able to.

She received care from a medical specialist, and I also gave her homeopathic remedies. There's no known cure for Crohn's, but various treatments can greatly ease the symptoms and make life more bearable for the sufferer. My remedies often provided relief, but not always, and her specialist also discussed the possibility of surgery. For over a decade, Husna managed to avoid surgery, but increasingly those in charge of her care advised that it was her best option. Indeed, it became unavoidable.

'I know it has to be done,' Husna would say. 'But when? How can I take the time off to have surgery when people are in need of my help?'

ONE OF HUSNA'S MANY VOLUNTEER roles was assisting women in childbirth. She was often called on to perform this important role, and it took its toll. It demanded long hours and an emotional labour in proportion to the mother's physical effort. Husna would often be with women for hours, even days, providing comfort and care. One night in October 2018, Husna returned exhausted from helping a woman to have her baby, and headed straight to bed to get some rest. But, in the early hours of the morning, she was awoken by horrific pain. I rushed her straight to the hospital, and her condition was so bad that the medical staff decided to operate as soon as she was stable. They removed part of her colon. It was a very serious operation.

Afterwards, she was in terrible pain. I gave her homeopathic remedies to complement the hospital's medicine, and soon she was able to come home to recover. And, as soon as she was able to, she was back at her voluntary work, helping others despite her own suffering and discomfort.

Not long after the operation, when she was still supposed to be resting, she received a phone call: another woman had gone into labour, and needed Husna.

'I need you to drive me there,' she insisted. Then, as we were en route, she said, 'Oh! Can you go a little slower? It's hurting.'

I did as I was told, even though I was concerned about her carrying on with her work when she was still in pain.

Husna's Crohn's forced her to slow down, but it did not stop her. I knew nothing would do that, so instead I just reminded her to rest. She knew I was right—that she had to take time to let her body heal—but that didn't mean she was able to listen to me. Her compulsion to help others often overrode her care for herself, even when she knew her own health was at risk.

Crohn's was cruel to Husna, but it could not make her cruel.

Instead, the cruelty of her disease turned her into a kinder person. It taught her to feel the pain of others even more than she already did.

Suffering causes many people in this world to become hard-hearted, but it had the opposite effect on Husna. Any loss, pain or suffering my wife experienced simply made her more sympathetic towards the suffering of others. It made her more motivated to offer comfort in whatever way she could. Like everything else in her life, her own physical suffering was something she accepted and embraced, moving past it to let it teach her how to be the best person she could be.

11.

Kindness

দয়া

DURING OUR VISIT HOME TO Bangladesh in 1997, Husna and I went to see one of her relatives. This relative lived a long way from Husna's village. To get there, we needed to travel first by bus, then take a boat.

When we got off the bus, we hired a boat driven by an old man. He reached out to take Husna's bags, intending to carry them to the boat as he did for all his customers, but Husna stopped him.

'No, please don't do that,' she said to him.

'You can trust me, *mam*,' he reassured her. 'I will not damage anything.'

Like many Bangladeshis, he had assumed that Husna was a foreigner because of her complexion. Even though she had been born in Bangladesh, local people would often be adamant she'd come from overseas and had learned to speak Bengali somehow. In New Zealand, we would meet Malaysians who were convinced Husna must have come from Malaysia. 'You stole one of ours!' they'd tease me.

Husna realised that the boatman thought she was suspicious of his intentions.

'You are an old man, and I should respect you like a father because I am young,' she explained to him. 'I can't allow you to carry my heavy bags at your age. You might hurt yourself, and I am perfectly capable of doing it myself.'

At her words, tears came to the boatman's eyes. 'I wish all young ladies were like you, my daughter!' he said. 'You are very kind. I am fortunate to be taking you in my boat today.'

The old boatman might have been poor, but he had a big heart. He tried to give Husna a discount for her kindness, but she refused. In fact, she went one better and forced him to take a greater fare than he'd initially quoted.

We set off in the boat, but the river was running high and the current rough. The boatman decided to take a course close to the riverbank. Soon, we came across a cow that was tied up on the bank, eating grass. Suddenly the land beneath the cow's hooves slipped away and the beast fell into the water, but the rope stayed firmly tied round its neck. Instead of being swept away, the cow dangled in the water's rushing flow, thrashing about and trying not to drown.

Husna began to shout out to the people on the riverbank nearby, trying to draw their attention to the distressed creature, but all they did was stare at her in shock. It was not customary for a young lady to behave like that in public, but Husna didn't care about that in her desire to see the cow rescued.

'My daughter! You should not scream!' said the boatman, interrupting her. 'Let me do it for you.'

This time the cow's owner heard the boatman's cries, and he rushed to save the animal just in time. The man was a poor villager and was so relieved that he thanked the boatman profusely.

'Do not thank me,' said the boatman, and he gestured to Husna. 'You should be thanking this kind-hearted woman. Ever since I met her, she has shown kindness after kindness.'

That was Husna. Everywhere she went, she managed to touch people's hearts with her kindness. It was innate, a quality she could not hide. She was the embodiment of love for others.

IN RECENT TIMES, MANY YOUNG families from Bangladesh have come to make Christchurch their home. Husband and wife will come here together if they can. If not, the man might come ahead of his wife, and she will follow once her paperwork for entering the country has been processed. Sometimes, a woman will become pregnant soon after arriving, or she might even already be pregnant when she comes here. She'll need help with her pregnancy and childbirth, and with navigating the medical system, but she might not speak much English. This is where Husna would step in.

Many of these women had husbands who worked full time, so they would turn to Husna for help. And, as you know, Husna could never say no. 'These women need something that I can give them,' she would say. 'Why would I refuse them?'

Husna kept a folder full of all the important information relating to the pregnant women and new mothers she was caring for. She kept records of everything—midwives' contact details, scan and test dates, hospital bookings, immunisation reminders, even the date of a baby's first haircut. She spent innumerable hours in person or on the phone giving advice and help, or driving women to and from various appointments. She would be with them when they laboured and gave birth, and would stay beside them afterwards to comfort and support them.

Of course, when you dedicate your time to helping others, you are bound to come across those who don't truly appreciate what you are doing. Some people are not grateful for the generosity that others show them. This never bothered Husna, because she gave for the sake of giving. She gave to earn God's blessing. She did not want to receive anything in return. If ever someone was openly ungrateful to her, she would simply say, 'That's OK. Their response has nothing to do with me. I give in the hope of being rewarded by Allah. To give truly, one does so without expecting anything in return.' It was a good philosophy, as it saved my wife from being hurt by the unkindness of others.

Through her selfless and tireless work with all these new mothers, Husna earned the love, respect and admiration of the women in the Bangladeshi community in Christchurch. To them she became a type of mother figure, someone to whom they could turn for advice, comfort, safety, love. The Bangladeshi community held Husna in extremely high esteem for her unwavering commitment to the well-being of their families.

A FEW YEARS AGO, HUSNA decided that it was time a dedicated Bengali class was held at the mosque for the Bangladeshi children. We still had our children's class on Islam, which was open to the international community, but Husna saw the need for Bangladeshi children to be taught Bengali as well so that they would retain their mother tongue. As well as teaching them about Islam in Bengali, she also wanted to include more general reading and writing activities, singing and cultural performances. So she created another class to that specific end—and also created a whole lot more work for herself, and for me! We were happy to take on these additional responsibilities, however, as we could see that the class was necessary.

Before long, it had also proved incredibly popular. Husna trained some other women to help her with teaching, and she expanded the class into a special children's programme that included getting the children to do performances in Bengali, much to the delight of the wider community. The children became incredibly attached to 'Aunty Husna'. They loved her, and she loved them.

12.

Love

ভালবাসা

HUSNA DREAMED OF BECOMING A mother. She knew she would be a good parent, and was hopeful that we would one day be blessed with a child, but she was also patient about her desire. There was no rush. Like me, she believed that the ultimate power lay in God's hands. It is Allah who decides who shall be a parent, and who shall not. So, together we prayed for His mercy, that He might grant us our wish, at the same time as accepting without complaint whatever His choice might be.

Although we faced more than a couple of impediments when it came to becoming parents—Husna's Crohn's and my disability, to name the two most obvious—we remained hopeful. In this instance, Husna set her tendency to worry aside by resting on her faith. She did not fret, because she surrendered to the will of Allah. We accepted our destiny, whatever shape it would take, and we let our faith guide us to be happy with the gifts that we had.

And then, in 2003, we learned we would be parents after all. Husna was pregnant—but it was not an easy pregnancy. Her Crohn's flared up repeatedly, and before long it became evident that the baby was growing more slowly than it should be. This was a cause for concern. I suggested to Husna's obstetrician that perhaps we could try one of my homeopathic remedies. 'Let's see if it works,' she said. 'If it doesn't, we'll try something else.' But we didn't need to resort to her backup plan, as my remedy did its job. At the next check-up, we were immensely relieved to learn that the baby's growth was back on track.

As the birth neared, Husna's obstetrician advised that a caesarean section would be the safest delivery option for both her and the baby. That meant surgery for Husna, but she welcomed it happily. The most important thing to her was becoming a mother, and protecting her child.

On 14 January 2004, we were admitted to Christchurch Hospital, and I was there in the operating theatre with Husna when our baby was born. One of the medical staff placed a solid, healthy girl in my arms. *Alhamdulillah!* Thanks be to Allah. I will never forget that day.

The little baby glared up at me. It was as though she were asking, 'And who are *you?*'

'*Ami tomar prio baba,*' I told my daughter. *I am your loving father.*

Then I passed her to her mother, so that Husna could hold her baby as soon as possible. Fat tears of joy rolled down my wife's cheeks. Her dream had come true. She was a mother. Our daughter was a precious gift from Allah, a miracle of life.

HUSNA'S CROHN'S CONSPIRED WITH HER caesarean surgery to make it painful and difficult for her to carry her newborn daughter about.

'That's no problem,' I said. 'I can carry our baby in my lap.'

So that's what we did. It worked very well for all three of us. Husna was a very protective mother, but she trusted me to wheel our daughter about, and that made me a very happy father. I found huge joy in my role as carrier of our baby: I wheeled her from room to room with me, and I sang to her from the Quran to put her to sleep. The task caused me back pain, but my enjoyment transcended that. All those years earlier in Burwood, I had worried that my accident had rendered me useless, and now here I was performing the most necessary of tasks as a father. I realised how ill-founded my fears had been. I was more than useful; I was needed.

Occasionally, Husna had to be hospitalised as a result of her Crohn's, and she was forced to leave our baby daughter at home with me. Husna was fastidious, and left me with clear instructions for how to prepare our daughter's milk and how to get her to sleep. I was not as naturally meticulous as Husna, so I had to make an effort to meet her standards in order to earn her trust and confidence. However, as she had right from the time of our engagement and marriage, she placed her trust unerringly in my hands. In parenthood, as in everything else, we made a good team.

Thank Allah for our daughter. Even as a baby, she was very calm, happy and undemanding. She would smile up at me from where she rested on my lap, and as she grew older she would play on and around my wheelchair. She enjoyed my singing and the sound of my prayers, and when we took her along to our children's classes at the mosque she would wait patiently and quietly. To this day, whenever people learn whose daughter she is, they will comment, 'Oh! Of course she is Husna's child. I am not surprised at all.'

IT TOOK US SOME TIME to agree upon a name for our little girl. As with everything else in life, Husna would settle for only the name that she felt was the best. My wife's perfectionism was an admirable trait, but it did not often make for easy answers! Whenever we made joint decisions, it took a lot of energy to convince Husna. She always made me think hard and interrogate everything, and this was never truer than when it came to naming our baby.

Husna assigned the task of finding a name to me. I'd helped lots of parents with finding names for their babies, so I thought it was going to be an easy job—but I'd obviously forgotten to factor in my wife's personality. Every name I came up with was rejected. Husna did not feel that any of the names I suggested were quite right; she wanted the *perfect* name. Soon, I began to question whether the name that would please my wife even existed, but I embraced the quest. If such a name did exist, I would find it! Searching was, in fact, quite fun and I learned a lot. Every time I came across a name I liked, I had to thoroughly describe its definitions to Husna, then she and I would debate its merits—and Husna would ultimately add it to the pile of discards.

Then, at long last, a name entered my mind that I liked very much. *Shifa*. Perhaps Husna would like this name as much as I did?

Shifa is an Arabic word meaning 'healing' or 'cure of sickness, suffering and discomfort'. I took the name to my wife and I explained my logic.

'Comforting others is one of your traits,' I said. 'If we name our daughter Shifa, that trait will be part of her personality too.'

Plus, I added, as well as being a beautiful name it is also a blessed one, since it's mentioned in the Holy Quran (17:82). I would also, I promised, name my business Shifa Homeopathic Clinic to tie in with the word's meaning.

At long last, my wife was convinced.

Our daughter had a name: Shifa Ahmed.

DUE TO THE EXTRAORDINARY SACRIFICE a mother makes for her child—in pregnancy, in childbirth and in rearing—our faith commands us to offer thrice the love and care to a mother that we do to a father. That's why the Prophet Muhammad (peace be upon him) rightly told a man who asked whom he should care for the most, 'Your mother.' When the man asked again, the Prophet repeated, 'Your mother.' When the man asked a third time, saying, 'Then whom, O Messenger of God?' the reply was yet again, 'Your mother.' Only when the man asked a fourth time did the answer change to, 'Then your father.' (Muttafaqun A'Laih)

The connection between a mother and her child is a sacred one, and the bond between Husna and her daughter was extremely close. Husna was the best of mothers. Her approach was always balanced between love and discipline. Our home has always been a place of calmness, and that serenity is reflected in our daughter's behaviour. Guided by her smile and her sense of humour, Husna would often joke and be silly with Shifa, but she was also strict about good manners and adhering to daily routines. Husna set the same high standards for her daughter as she set for herself and for me. She always wanted all of us to do our best, and she encouraged Shifa to achieve in her studies and in her religious practice.

Every day, Shifa asked her mother the same thing: 'Amma, do you love me?'

She'd then wait eagerly to hear the response, even though she already knew what it would be. It was always the same.

'Yes,' Husna would reply, smiling. 'I do love you, *pakhi*.'

Pakhi means bird, and it was just one of many special names that Husna had for her daughter. She would invent silly little nicknames that had no real meaning—things like *mukuli* or *putuly*—but Shifa and I always understood what they meant. They were an expression of a mother's love and affection.

Husna loved Shifa truly and totally, in a way that only a mother can. However, she did not love her blindly. Her love for her child resided in her desire to care for and guide Shifa, not to spoil her.

'Spoiling my child would harm her in the future,' Husna would say.

She taught Shifa to value human qualities over material gains. Shifa has inherited her mother's capacity to be happy with and thankful for the gifts she has, to be frugal, and to be kind to those in need. Our daughter, like her mother, has many friends who turn to her for counsel or support when they are facing hardship. Husna always encouraged Shifa to welcome her friends into our home, so that they might share our food and enjoy Husna's delicious cooking.

Husna was an exceptional mother, but she was always humble. When others praised her daughter, Husna would just smile and thank Allah for her child. The most powerful way that my wife taught our daughter was through her own good example. She never enforced rules upon Shifa that she herself did not practise. As a result, she empowered our daughter to make her own moral judgements and decisions. Shifa has worn her headscarf since preschool, as she saw her mother wearing hers all the time.

Husna instilled a sense of independence in our daughter from a very young age, teaching her to read early, but she was also as protective as any mother. In fifteen years, she barely slept at night, always keeping an ear out in case her daughter should need her.

HUSNA WAS ONLY EIGHT MONTHS old when her own mother died, and from time to time my wife used to say to me that she thought she would die young too. I used to dismiss the idea, as I thought it was more likely that I would go before her. I am twelve years older than Husna, after all, and with my accident my physical well-being took an irreparable hit. It seemed incredible that I would outlive my positive, strong wife, even factoring in her battles with Crohn's disease.

Even so, every time Husna found herself in hospital due to a Crohn's flare-up, she would be convinced she was going to die. She would give me a list of things I was supposed to tell our daughter and—even though it was grief upon grief for me—I would listen quietly and try to reassure her. 'Don't worry, Husna!' I'd say. 'Allah will look after us and Shifa.'

Then she'd call Shifa, giving her a list of instructions too.

'Amma! I am doing fine,' Shifa would reply. 'You just concentrate on getting better, and soon.'

But Husna could not help it, could not make herself stop. Her role as a mother compelled her to worry about us. She wanted to make sure we were taken care of, even if she was not there to do the job herself.

IT WAS NEVER STRANGE FOR us to talk about death together. According to our faith, both Husna and I believe that wisdom lies in retaining an awareness of our own mortality. Remembering that we die is a way to remind ourselves to be humble, conscious of others and thankful for every second of life that God gives us. We often talked about death together at the dinner table, Shifa included, and would discuss what the duties would be of those who survived if one of us should be taken from this life. Our daughter was part of these conversations because we wanted to help her prepare for the day that happened.

Allah alone knows when we are to die, so we were cautious and did what we could to prepare, then we left the rest with Him. We knew, as the Holy Quran tells us, that 'to Allah we belong, and truly to Him is our return' (2:156). So, we surrendered our fate to Allah without worries.

Naturally, we were hopeful that we might have many more years together ahead of us. We did not expect death to come to our home so soon, or in such a way as it did, and certainly not to Husna.

Who could possibly have prepared for such a thing?

Who could have known that Husna's prediction would ultimately come to pass?

A BULLET CAN END A human's life, but it cannot kill love. Love is immortal. It is inscribed in stone. Indelible. No one can remove it. The love that Husna had for me and the love that she had for our daughter lives on in us. It is alive in our memories. It is alive in the memories of all those who felt the warm rays of my wife's goodness and generosity in her 44 years on this earth with us.

Love survives.

Love is divine.

Love is pure.

III

The worst
of acts

13.

Before

AS I FAREWELL MY WIFE and enter Masjid al-Noor, my main
concern is not disturbing those worshippers who have arrived
before me. Since I use a wheelchair, I tend to go in through the
back entrance, as it allows me to enter the main prayer room by way
of the smaller men's room first.

I know that, inside the main room, men will already be seated
on the carpeted floor. Worshippers pick their spots on a first
come, first served basis, filling up the front row first, according to
mosque protocols. This is the biggest room in the mosque, and it's
from this room that the imam delivers his sermon and leads the
congregation. The other, smaller men's room provides extra space if
the main room is ever too full. The women and children have their

own room for worship, out of respect and to give them privacy. In this room, they can hear the imam's sermon over the microphone system and watch it on a large TV. This is the room my wife has gone to.

Despite my earlier delays with the knot in the tassel on my trousers, I have managed to arrive not too late. As I enter the smaller room, those who are already here kindly make way for me. There are a number of men in here, sitting quietly or reciting the Holy Quran. As usual, I greet everyone I see. Most of these people know me because I have been a part of this community for almost 21 years, not only worshipping here but teaching weekly classes with Husna and often delivering Friday sermons or lectures.

I'm planning to go into the main room and take my usual spot, on the right-hand end of the front row. From there, I'll be able to clearly hear Imam Gamal Fouda's sermon, and will also be able to wait to leave last, so as not to disturb the prayers of the other worshippers.

However, as I move towards the door to the main room, a man sitting in a nearby chair catches my eye, and I pause.

I know this man, and have done for many years. He is a retired university professor, and just a few weeks ago he told me devastating news: he has been diagnosed with cancer, and the prognosis is not good.

He is quietly praying, and my heart goes out to him.

Will I see him again next Friday? I wonder. It is impossible to know.

I go over to hug him and to make *du'a* (prayer) for his health. I want to spend a little time with him before the imam's sermon begins. He is happy to see me, as I am to see him, and we greet each other in low voices then talk together quietly before resuming our prayers. In the back of my mind, I'm also aware of the time, and I'm thinking that I should start making my way into the main prayer room.

However, my thoughts are interrupted by a sound: *azan*, the call to prayer.

Soon, the imam will begin his sermon. I decide to sit and wait beside my sick friend until it is finished. I do not want to disrupt the worshippers already in the main room by wheeling my chair in while the imam is speaking. I can still hear the sermon from here, and I'm happy to wait in this small room, safe with the other worshippers.

The imam begins his sermon in Arabic, then after about five minutes switches to English. While he speaks, everyone is quiet, giving him their full attention. Listening to this sermon is an important part of Jumu'ah. The mosque is infused with a serenity born of the worshippers' attentiveness and respect. Everyone has come here today in search of spiritual happiness through shared prayer. It is calm, hopeful. Peaceful.

Guided by the atmosphere in the room and by the imam's words, I listen closely and focus my own thinking. I concentrate on fixing the advice from the Holy Quran and the Prophet (peace be upon him) firmly in my mind, so that I might use it to be a better person, someone who will offer goodness to this world through my own actions.

But my prayers and the sense of peace in the room are ruptured by an awful sound.

It comes from somewhere near the mosque's main entrance. The sound cuts the imam's voice in two, tearing through our quiet worship.

I recognise that sound. It is the sound of gunfire.

In that moment, our most sacred of places becomes a site of chaos and fear.

14.

During

ALARM FLOODS MY BODY. THE sound of shooting keeps coming, but because I am in the men's room, down the hall from the mosque's entrance, I can't see what is happening.

At first, I wonder if someone is playing an awful trick. *Is it a toy gun? Or is it . . .*

My mind cannot go there, cannot consider that the gun might be real, but every second that ticks by pulls me closer to the truth of things. Worry begins to seep in, along with horror.

The imam's sermon suddenly stops.

People begin to run into the smaller men's room, then race out of the building through the door near me. Their eyes are wide, full of fear. They look as though they are running for their lives. They are panicking. They want to get out, but there are not many doors into and out of the mosque. Besides the main entrance, there's also the door out of this room and another door on the other side of the building. Otherwise, there are only windows.

In their desperation to get outside, to get away, people push past me. Blinded by their desire to escape, they barely notice a man in his wheelchair, but I am more worried about their safety than I am about my own.

What is happening? The question bounces about in my head, but I fail to latch on to the answer. *What is going on?*

Then, as the answer finally clicks into place, the question changes. *Why?*

That word freezes me to the spot. I cannot move, cannot offer help.

All I can think is, *Why is this happening? Who would do this to us, in such a sacred place and on such a holy day?*

Within moments, the exit door is jammed with people. They press themselves against one another, frantically trying to get out even if there are others in the way. They push and pull at one another's bodies, not realising what they are doing, not realising that they are hurting each other. Some fall to the floor, and are held there by the urgent press of those running over them. They rush past me, and still I don't move. I want them to get out ahead of me, want them to live.

The room is filled with panic and with movement, but draped across it I feel a heavy silence, pierced only by the sound of gunfire. I can't hear any sound. I do not notice screaming, yelling, crying. Inside my head, it is as quiet as death.

I see some people streaked with blood. Some are limping. That is when I know, for certain, what is happening here.

I REMAIN WHERE I AM, watching all the people going past me, their faces filled with fear. They all have one aim: to get outside as fast as they can. My mind is clouded with thoughts of death, and with them come thoughts of life, too. These thoughts rush and clamour like the people around me, punctuated by the sound of gunfire.

My thoughts go so quickly that it's difficult to rest on one before another swoops in to take its place. I have no idea how many shooters there are, but I'm guessing from the blood I'm seeing on the people trying to escape that a shooter has gone into the main men's room, and will probably come into this smaller room soon. I see death's face, and I presume it is coming for me today. The outside door is now completely blocked with people desperately trying to get out; there is no way I will fit through there in my wheelchair. Even if I could get through the door, it's unrealistic to hope that I'd get very far before a bullet caught up with me.

I think of Husna. Where is she? Has she got out?

And then, my worst fear: Has a shooter gone into the women's and children's room?

Even as these thoughts whirl through my mind, I am alert. I am calm. I look down at my hands. They are steady. I do not call out. I simply watch, and I wait.

I surrender myself to the will of Allah. I do as the prophet Abraham (peace be upon him) did in the Holy Quran—when asked to surrender everything to Allah, he replied happily, and without complaint or hesitation, 'I bow [my will] to the Lord and Cherisher of the Universe.' (2:131) Doing the same now helps me to be calm, to not be scared.

I am, however, deeply unsettled. Both happiness and sadness course through me. Happiness because, if I do die today, I know that Allah will grant me a place in Paradise for my innocence. My faith in the next life gives me hope. But I'm also sad when I think of my wife and my daughter. *If I am killed*, I wonder, *will they suffer without me?*

'Farid!' I tell myself. 'If death embraces you today, be happy. Do not complain. Let us presume today is your last day. How do you feel about that?'

My heart and mind reply together, 'If that is the wish of my Lord Allah, then so be it.'

But my thoughts keep swinging back round to my wife, and I do not like to dwell on where she might be, what might be happening to her. I quickly block out those thoughts by putting hope in their place.

Insha Allah, she will be OK. God willing. She is a smart woman.

SOON, THE ROOM IS COMPLETELY empty. I look at the exit door, and I see that it is now clear. The direction of my thoughts alters. Now, alongside the option of staying where I am to await my fate sits another: I can go outside and try to get away.

A part of me questions the point in bothering. 'You're going to die anyway,' it says. But there is another part of me, the part guided by Islam and by wisdom, that reminds me, 'If you do not at least try to live, you will lose your place in Paradise. Waiting here for death would be akin to suicide, which is a sin prohibited by your Lord Allah in the Holy Quran.'

If I am killed trying to escape, I know I will be allowed into Paradise. If I somehow survive, Allah will have granted me more time to continue doing good for others—a gift He also granted 21 years ago when I survived my accident, even though my doctors did not think I would.

So, slowly and deliberately, I begin to wheel my chair towards the exit. I can still hear the sound of gunfire, and with every push I expect a bullet to rip through the back of my head, but I carry on. (Later, a man who saw me as he fled will say, 'I saw you pushing yourself out, and you were doing it so gently, it made me angry. I wanted to yell at you to hurry up and get away as fast as possible.')

As I go, I consider where I will hide, if I get the chance.

My car is parked outside, at the end of the ramp, but the robotic arm that stows my wheelchair takes a couple of minutes to do its job. That is too long. My car is too close to the mosque for that. I do not think I have a couple of minutes.

Behind my car is a smaller building, but I already know I won't be able to go in there. It will probably be locked, and even if it isn't there's no wheelchair access.

I could keep pushing myself to try to get further away, but it won't be long before the concrete runs out and my wheelchair is brought to a standstill by grass or pebbles.

In another direction is a high wall, and I see others flinging themselves over it. That is, obviously, not an option for me.

All the while my thoughts are torn and muddled by the ongoing sounds of shooting from within the mosque. My thinking is not very organised. How could it be? Thoughts burst into my mind like flashes of lightning, each one disappearing as another comes along.

I decide to hide behind my car. From there, I might be able to help anyone who comes past me. I also hope that my dear wife might come this way, looking for me.

When I get behind my car, I see a man I know called Naseem Khan. He is originally from Bangladesh, like me, and he is hiding behind the small storeroom near the wall.

'Come over here!' he whispers to me. 'You might get spotted there. You might get shot.'

Meanwhile, worshippers continue to flee over the high wall, but Naseem does not go anywhere.

'Run away!' I tell him. 'Jump over the wall!'

'How can I leave you?' he responds. 'My heart will not allow me to do that. Look, if we die today, we will both die.'

His presence is an enormous comfort to me. I admire his love and courage. He is a hero to me.

I ask him many times over about my wife, and about the other women and children. 'What is happening to them? Do you know?'

I do not have a phone, and I ask Naseem if he knows if anyone has called an ambulance or the police. He isn't sure.

The gunfire is intermittent, but whenever it stops it soon starts again. Every time I hear it, it feels as though bullets are ripping through my own heart. I can do nothing here besides think, and I feel utterly helpless. I am praying for it to cease. When the sound stops, I feel a small moment of hope—but then it just starts again, and the pain comes rushing back.

I cannot work out what is happening. Why is the gunfire

stopping and starting like that? Is everyone inside dead? If they are, why is the shooter still firing?

I am filled with concern for my wife. I know her so well that I am certain she will not run away to save herself if there are others who need her help. I am so worried about her, but I'm not close enough to the women's and children's room to have any idea what is going on in there, if anything. Would a shooter go in there? Is Husna OK? What can I do?

Sitting here in my wheelchair, unable to do anything, only makes these thoughts all the more terrible. I can do nothing to silence them, to distract myself from them. If I could at least do something, I could focus on that, but my wheelchair limits my ability to help in any physical way.

Every moment is a lifetime.

I do my best not to panic, not to scream, not to cry. I remain calm, but I am also in agony. In my mind, I pray to Allah for the best outcome. I hope help from outside will arrive soon. Someone must have called emergency services by now. Where are the police? An ambulance? Anything.

As I wait, my mind touches on each of the people I know who could still be inside the mosque. From time to time, I picture the imam's face, and I worry about what might have happened to him. From where he was standing in his high mimbar, and as a religious leader, I imagine he would have been an immediate target to a shooter walking into the main prayer room. He wouldn't have been able to run away. His sermon stopped so abruptly—why? Thinking about our imam and what might have happened to him renders me weak and hopeless, but I try to push away the feeling with my prayers. I have delivered sermons at our mosque so many times. What if it had been me in the imam's place today?

I also know that there would have been people of all ages in the main prayer room—the elderly, the ill, the very young. Perhaps younger people might have been able to run away, but what of the sick and frail? What of the children? Would a shooter target them, or spare them? The mere thought that the young, the old, the sick would not be shown mercy chills me.

Still, I pray. I try to console my heart, to retain hope.

I am beginning to understand that people have been killed today. There's no avoiding that fact, not now. Grief cloaks me, as my mind leaps forward to the future, to what death means for those who are left behind.

I know, too, that there will be people who are injured. They will be in pain, suffering. I imagine them crying out for help, filled with shock and fear. Some of them will already be feeling death's cold fingers reaching for them, grasping at their edges. If an ambulance doesn't arrive soon, they will die too. I don't know why there is still no ambulance. Why is it taking so long? Every second stretches out painfully before me.

As I think of all the others, I am also thinking of my wife. I am waiting to see her escape, hoping she might come and join me out here by our car. Where is she? Is she looking for me? I wish I could go and find her myself, tell her where I am.

I am caught in a struggle between hopelessness and hope, but I do not feel angry—not even when I think of the killer. There might be one shooter, or more, I still don't know. I am terrified, but even so I am able to thank Allah: I am grateful that I am not a killer like whoever has done this. I feel immense sadness when I think about the perpetrator of such horror. I know that, in taking the precious lives of innocent people, they have simply destroyed their own innocence. I wish they understood that, in harming others, they have harmed themselves.

What benefit could there possibly be in killing other people? None.

What peace could someone possibly achieve in their heart, and in the hearts of others, by taking the lives of a group of worshippers? None.

Thinking of the horror and pain that murder sows further saddens me. There will be a reaction to this. What form will it take? Will there be retaliation? More bloodshed? I pray not. The idea fills me with fear.

I am not frightened for the sake of my own life. I am frightened for our world, for our future. I know that acts like this deliberately threaten the things we should all hold most dear: peace, harmony, unity, stability. What is this going to mean for Kiwi Muslims? What is this going to mean for our children? What will happen to our schools, our jobs, our mosques, our places of sanctuary and safety? In my mind's eye, I can see how far the dark shadow of this attack might stretch. It is poisonous, truly terrifying.

I pray for New Zealand, for this country that has shown me and my family so much love. This is my home. It is Husna's home. It is our daughter's home, the place where she came into the world. Will my family be OK after today? Will we, as Muslims, still be safe here, in our home?

How will our government respond? Will our politicians take

Muslim citizens seriously? Will they understand and acknowledge what has happened here? And what of our fellow Kiwis? Will they feel sad? Will they show their Muslim brothers and sisters love, show us support?

These questions multiply and expand, filling my mind until there are too many to fit, but they keep coming and they all demand to be heard. I cannot know the answer to any of them, so I try to quieten them with prayer. I try to quell my fear with hope.

And then I notice that the gunfire has stopped. I wait, and it does not start again.

15.
After

I WAIT. ONE MINUTE. TWO. More. Several minutes pass and still there is no sound of gunfire. The shooter, or shooters, must have left. At least, I presume that's the case. I am guessing whoever did this would not stick around for long after they were done. It's time for me to go back inside.

I whisper to Naseem, who is still nearby, and tell him my intentions.

'I'm coming with you,' he says.

So together, in the name of Allah, we begin to move towards the mosque.

It is hope that compels me to take this risk. I am aware that the shooter may not have left at all, may yet have other awful plans, but

I do not worry about that. I also know that, most likely, what awaits me inside is not something I want to see. I try to prepare myself for the worst, because that is surely what I am about to discover. The shooting went on for long enough that I know the chances of survival for anyone in the mosque are slim. The people inside will be my friends and acquaintances, people I know and with whom I worship and share my life. I know their faces. I do not want to see them harmed, disfigured, dead.

I am also driven inside by concern for my wife. I still have not seen Husna, and I can't stop thinking about her, or the other women and children. I cannot wait out here knowing that people I know and love might be inside, alone, afraid.

So I go in because I must. If there are people inside who need help, I may be able to provide some spiritual assistance, may be able to do some good. If there is anyone inside who is dying, I can recite the shahada (declaration of faith) for them. If there is anyone who is injured, I can talk to them, maybe give them at least a little hope. At last, after being forced to hide beside my car, I can do something. My body held me back while the shooting was happening, but my mind liberates me to return now. I must use my mental and emotional abilities to help in some way. They are my strength.

This is what hope does: it gives you the courage to return to a site of horror so that you might treat the wound with love.

WHEN I LEFT THE MOSQUE, I had wheeled myself calmly and slowly. Now, I am pushing my chair forward as fast as I can. I am in a hurry to get inside. My heart is racing.

Just before Naseem and I go inside, we encounter a man. He is still alive, but he is screaming in agony. I see his leg is injured, and I learn that he was shot as he tried to get out of the mosque. I do what I can to console him, to reassure him that help will come soon, then I carry on.

My worry for Husna is peaking. If she is inside, will she be alive? The thought that she might not be is unbearable to me. I'm desperate to know where she is. I feel so guilty about having been forced to hide by my car, about having been unable to come inside sooner. If she has been in here protecting others, I wish I could have been there doing the same for her. If she is still in here now, I must join her as soon as I can.

I go in through the same door by which I left: the door into the smaller men's room. The room is silent, but I do not look around. I keep going forward, desperate to get to the women's and children's room. To get there, I have to pass through the door to the library and then through the kitchen door.

In the last two decades, I have gone through these doors more times than I can count. Usually, I come through them, then knock on the door to the women's room, and whoever answers will, upon seeing me, immediately call out to Husna. It often takes a minute for Husna to appear—she is always busy attending to someone else, and will finish whatever she is doing before she leaves. Now, though, I am not expecting anyone to answer the door or to call my wife's name. Even if someone is on the other side, it's unlikely they'll answer, out of fear. I am expecting the very worst, balanced on a wire strung between fear and hope.

I reach the door and I knock.

As I suspect, there's no response.

I knock again, and again.

Still nothing.

So, my heart thumping and my mind fuzzy, I open the door. I look inside. The room is empty. There is no one in here.

Momentary relief floods my heart. The women and children must have managed to run away while the shooter was in the main prayer room.

So where is Husna? I am hopeful that, since she's not here, she might be safe somewhere. She will come back to me once everything has settled down.

This thought reassures me. I leave my wife's care in the hands of God, and I decide to check the other rooms too. I want to help any others who might be in here. I know that's what Husna would do.

AS I MAKE MY WAY towards the main prayer room, I take in everything I can. My eyes dart from detail to detail, never resting in one place for long before moving on to the next thing. The more I see, the more I realise the true extent of this attack. It is heartbreaking. It is unfathomable. It spurs me on, urges me to move faster.

I go back through the library and into the main prayer room. The big folding door is wide open, but even so I have trouble getting into the main room because there are bodies everywhere. I struggle to manoeuvre my wheelchair around them, frantically searching for anyone who might still be alive.

On the ground near the door that leads from the entrance hallway into the main room I notice something else: empty bullet shells. There are a lot of them lying within a relatively small area. Is this where the killer stood? If so, it looks as though they stayed in this one spot for a while. From here, they would have been able to see anyone who tried to lunge their way, and they would have been able to take aim at any and all of the innocent people who were worshipping when they stormed in.

I see that many—far too many—of the bullets have found their mark. All around, there are dead bodies. The destruction fans out from the scattered shells. None of these people would have expected a person to arrive, their soul tarred with hate, to shoot them dead while they prayed. The worshippers had all come here in peace. Such cruelty has caught them off guard, and taken their lives as its toll.

I notice that some windows are broken, so perhaps some people managed to escape, but I can see that others died trying. The devastation is total. There are bodies on the floor, on the sofa, in the middle of the room and at its edges. There are bodies on bodies, some of them facing down and shot from behind. It is so silent.

Never before could I have imagined that someone could do something like this. Why would I? It is unthinkable. This sort of brutality has no place in a peaceful soul.

I push my chair towards the imam's mimbar. He is not there, but another man is. I recognise the caller of the prayer lying dead on the floor, a man who is—or was—a retired academic. He studied for his PhD at Lincoln University. He was sitting on a chair in front of the imam, but his body has slumped to the floor.

I turn to the right, gazing towards the spot where I usually pray on Fridays, and there I see more dead bodies. There are more on this side of the room than anywhere else. The only reason I wasn't here when the shooter arrived is because I stopped to pray with my sick friend. Now, among the dead piled where I might have been, I recognise some of the elderly people I usually sit next to. Some bodies are piled upon others, as though people were trying to get out over the top of the dead when they, too, were shot.

Nearby, on a sofa, I recognise another man. Held tight in his arms is his son. They are both dead. Their love for one another survives in their embrace. Even in death, the father is trying to protect his son from a horror he could never have foreseen. They look at peace, beneath the blood, but my bones are heavy with a sorrow unlike any other.

I wish I was not seeing this. I will never unsee it.

I hear screaming, and I turn towards it.

It is a man not far from me, and his legs are pinned in place by the body of another. He has been shot, is bleeding, and the weight of the dead man only adds to his pain.

'Please!' he cries out. 'Please, help me! I can't take any more!'

Beside him, facing the wall, is another man. 'I can't speak much,' this man says feebly, and I realise he is still alive too. 'Could someone please help the brother beside me?'

Hearing his voice, tears prick my eyes. I know this man as well. He is a retired university lecturer, a senior leader in our mosque, and has given many sermons here over the years. Often, I have taken his place if he has been unable to deliver a sermon. Seeing him now, shot and weak, yet still calling for help on behalf of others, I am extremely moved.

He cannot see me, and I do not want to further exhaust him by making him talk to me, so I say nothing. I want to go to help him and the other man, but I cannot. Between us lies an impenetrable barrier of bodies. I will never breach it, not in my wheelchair, and my heart fills with pain.

Then I spot Naseem. He is nearby, busy searching for anyone who might still be alive. He is checking the bodies of the dead to see who he knows. I call to him, and point towards the two men.

'Our injured brother needs someone to free his leg,' I say.

Naseem hesitates. 'I'm not sure I can do it on my own,' he says, but I encourage him to try.

When he eventually succeeds, the injured man breathes a sigh of relief. He is still in agony, but he thanks Naseem and prays for him. Even buried in horror and pain, our wounded brother has not lost his kindness.

Yet more injured lie among the dead, and I go to them in turn. There is not a lot I can do for those who are already close to death, but I do what I can. I offer comfort. I pray for them.

The next man I find alive is young, and he is having difficulty breathing.

'Brother, help me to sit up,' he says to me.

'I wish I could,' I reply, 'but I do not want to cause you further harm. Can you wait for the ambulance to arrive? The paramedics will know what they are doing. I do not.'

He is in a lot of pain, and I guide him to focus on Allah. This amazing young man does his best to smile at me, even through his distress. I quietly pray for him, and I move on to the next person.

Here is a man who is lying quietly, but his face is taut with suffering. He is bleeding badly.

'Thank God!' he says when he sees me. 'You are alive!'

'How are you, brother?' I ask him.

'*Alhamdulillah*,' he replies. *Thanks be to Allah.*

He is in immense pain, but his faith gives him strength. He expresses gratitude to our God, without complaint, despite his injury. I am humbled by his humility.

'Is an ambulance on the way?' he asks me.

'Yes,' I reply. Help cannot be far off now, I hope.

He falls quiet again, his face grim, and I move on.

I go back through the library and return to the smaller men's room, and here I find two more men I know. They are lying on their stomachs halfway out the door, their legs in the main prayer room while their heads are in the smaller room. It appears they have dragged themselves here, trying to get to the exit door, but have not been able to make it any further. The extent of their injuries and the attendant agony has brought them to a halt. One of them is a fellow Bangladeshi.

'*Bhai, ami shesh*,' he says when he sees me. *Brother, I am finished.*

'No way!' I reply in Bengali. 'You will be OK.'

'I am meant to go to Bangladesh tonight,' he tells me. 'With my pregnant wife and our two children. We are going to see my sick mother. She is waiting for me, but now I won't make it.'

'Do not worry,' I try to reassure him. 'You will go home soon to see your mum. For now, just focus on healing. Be positive and pray.'

The man next to him is someone I see often. He always prays beside me in the main prayer room. He is bleeding profusely.

'Good to see you alive, Brother Farid,' he says. 'Thank Allah!'

All of these injured men I have spoken to have expressed the same thing: they thank Allah that I am alive. Even in their agony, struggling for their own survival, these men retain the capacity to smile at me. They are happy to see me unharmed. It gives them hope. Able-bodied people were at least able to run, but not me, not in my wheelchair—and, yet, here I am. I have survived. These men are dying, but they do not envy me my life. Instead, it gives them joy. Hovering in that space between this life and the next, they are honest with me, and their honesty is expressed as love. This love is a precious gift. I keep it close, bring it into my own heart, even as it causes me immense distress.

'How are you?' I ask the man who usually prays beside me.

'I cannot move,' he replies. 'I would like some water. Are you able to bring me a glass?'

'Sure,' I say. 'I shall manage.'

I call Naseem, who is still in the other room, and he brings our injured brother a glass of water.

'Here it is,' I tell my friend. 'So long as the paramedics say it's OK for you to drink it when they arrive, it is all yours.'

'Thank you,' he says. 'One more thing. Are you able to remove my belt and tie it round my leg to stop the bleeding?'

'I've got a better idea,' I reply. 'I'll use my scarf. That way you won't have to move.'

It is as I'm removing my scarf that I hear a furious shout. I turn to see armed police storming into the room.

Two of them stride over to me, guns held firmly in their clenched fists.

'What are you doing here?' one of them says. His voice is very loud.

'You should not be in here. It's not safe,' the other adds. 'You need to leave immediately.'

Their eyes dart anxiously from me to Naseem to our grisly surrounds. They are trying to take it all in, and they are on their guard.

'I had to come back inside to see if I could help,' I say, trying to explain.

'What were you thinking?' one of them asks.

I understand their concern perfectly. I am a father and a teacher, so I know what it's like to worry for another person's safety. Indeed, I've often had to ask the same question of my students and, as a father, it is my duty to guide my child to act with wisdom. In the eyes of these police officers, I've taken a reckless risk. Why would I do something so unwise? Why would I willingly put myself in such danger?

The answer is simple: in a crisis situation, you do what you must, even if that means acting against the advice you'd usually give. I know full well that I have put my life on the line by coming back into our mosque, but what else could I have done? When offered the opportunity to return to the side of the injured and the dying, I had to take it. I could not flee and leave those who have so often listened to my sermons, in which I have preached about putting the needs of others first. I had to put my own words into practice. And, in truth, I am not afraid for my own life. If I am meant to die, then I will die. Until that day comes, I must act in a way that gives my heart peace, and that means helping those who need it, even if doing so jeopardises my own safety.

I do not mind the police officers' reprimands. I know they are speaking out of a desire to protect me. Their actions are born of love, not hate.

I have been making such an effort to hold on to my sense of hope that my positive spirit infuses my response to them. I smile at them, trying to lighten their worries by keeping my own manner light—but they don't respond to my cheerfulness.

I understand that they're not yet at a place where they can summon a smile amid a situation that seems so hopeless. I can see that they are reeling from the scene of devastation that they've walked into. Their own hearts and minds are struggling to make sense of such horror.

One of the police officers indicates that he wants me to get back outside by way of the exit door in the smaller men's room.

'Hurry, hurry!' he urges. 'Move, move!'

But I cannot hurry. If I go any faster than I already am, I will fall out of my wheelchair.

He calls Naseem over, and says, 'Help him get out of here. Push his wheelchair quickly. I'll guard you both while you get out.'

The police officer's anxiety is obvious, and I can almost read his thoughts. He seems to be anticipating that more will go wrong, preparing for things to get worse. His mind must be racing—it's his job to keep others safe, including me, and he's stressed that I might come to harm. I do everything in my power to comply with his urgency, and all the while I'm feeling my hope grow. Here we are, in the midst of the horror and death that hate reaps, and this officer is responding with love of the most selfless sort. He is shielding my life with his own, so that I won't be hurt. Even the most hateful action cannot take away my hope so long as people like this police officer exist. His generosity and concern for my safety is remarkable. He is also a hero to me.

I thank him, but I never get a chance to ask his name.

While Naseem pushes, I push too, in order to keep my balance.

As we pass my car, I ask the officer, 'Can I get my car?'

'Forget about your car!' he replies. 'You need to get out of here as fast as possible. It is not safe here.'

We leave through the back of the mosque, then make our way towards the front. There are bodies out here, too. I recognise some of them. I do not see my wife.

We do not stop.

We head towards the side gate. There is another gate out the front of the mosque, in the centre, but we don't go that way. We keep going, out through the side gate, and suddenly we are on the footpath of Deans Avenue.

We are outside.

Husna on her wedding evening in January 1994, getting some assistance with her dress from a Bangladeshi lady who lived in Auckland.

Farid helping Husna in the kitchen of their home in Nelson.

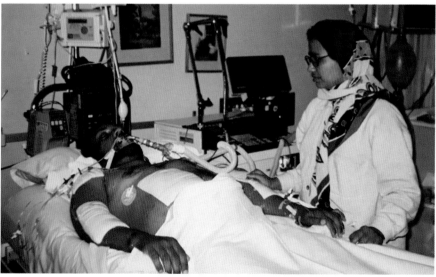

above Husna (centre right) with
colleagues outside Independent
Casing Co Ltd in Nelson, where
she worked as a machinist.

below Husna at Farid's bedside
in the intensive care unit at
Christchurch Hospital after he was
run over by a drunk driver, 1998.

Husna and Farid
with a young Shifa at
Bishopdale Park in
Christchurch.

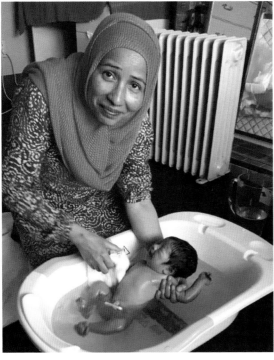

Many new parents
benefited from Husna's
gentle teaching. Here
she demonstrates how to
wash a newborn baby.

above Young performers and parents gather around Husna (centre) on the stage at a Bengali Language Day celebration.

right Ready to assist at another childbirth: Husna (right) with one of the staff members at Christchurch Women's Hospital.

left Husna supervises the serving of food at a Bangladeshi gathering.

below Special guest Lianne Dalziel (then Minister of Immigration) joins Husna at a large children's event in the early 2000s.

above Husna takes the microphone to lead her young students through a cultural performance.

right A quiet moment for Husna as she cuddles a newborn after assisting with a caesarean delivery at Christchurch Women's Hospital.

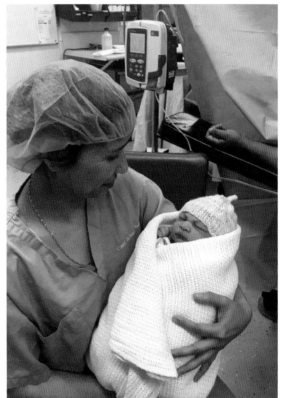

left Husna at home with Farid, who is holding Fareeha, their niece. The couple took the young girl and her mother, Fatima, into their home after the loss of Husna's beloved brother Kauser Ahmed to leukaemia in mid-2018.

below Fun at the park: Husna (left) with her sister-in-law Fatima and her niece Fareeha.

Husna and Farid at their home in Hoon Hay, Christchurch, on Qurbani Eid day in 2018. This is the last photo taken of Husna.

16.
Outside

ON THE FOOTPATH, IT IS chaos. Inside the mosque, everything was shrouded in the silence that accompanies death and suffering, but out here it is all noise and all movement. People are crying and yelling, others are speaking into their phones, sirens are wailing. The traffic is gridlocked. Some people are running frantically from one place to another, while others have fallen to the ground.

I meet the frenzy with calmness. I immediately see people I know, and we thank Allah for finding one another alive. Even though my heart is heavy, I greet each of them with a smile. I am determined to do what I can to encourage others, to try to provide a small amount of solace. Thinking of others helps me to carry on, to keep my own emotions in check.

At the forefront of my mind is Husna, and I am scanning the crowd for my lovely wife. I am hoping that she is already out here, searching for me too, but I do not see her. I try to find someone who might know where she is. I spot a couple of younger people who knew her, and I ask if they have seen her. 'No, no,' they tell me.

I am ushered along with some others to shelter behind a wall, but then the police deem that this is not safe enough and they move us further away. The footpath is rough and uneven, and it is difficult for me to navigate in my wheelchair. At one point I almost fall, but someone catches me and pulls me backwards, then tries to help by pushing me, but they don't know how to push a person in a wheelchair very well. I have to tell them what to do. Where is Husna? If she were here, she would push me herself. She would make sure that I was comfortable, unhurt. My back begins to ache, and every jolt and bump exacerbates both the pain and the absence of my wife. I hope I find her soon.

I want to stop, but I know I must keep moving. Now that I am outside the mosque, I am being more careful of my safety. Inside, when I was surrounded by the dead and dying, the thought of my own death did not frighten me. Now, however, I am outside and back in the company of the living. I have been reminded about life, and I am propelled by the urge to live. My thoughts are of my wife and my daughter. I have survived so far, and I need to stay alive for their sake. They will be waiting for me, worried about me.

All around me, other people are rushing to safety. They want to live too. They surge past me and alongside me and I am swept along with them. I see a man who was inside the mosque during the shooting. His shirt is stained red, but I don't think it's his blood. I ask him about what he saw, trying to get a better idea of what happened, but he is badly shaken. As he tells me what he witnessed, yet more sadness seeps into my soul.

The police keep asking us to move. Further away, then further still. I start to wonder what the point of it all is. They are just pushing us on along the same road. I am exhausted, but I remind myself that they are concerned for our safety. They are only doing what they think is best. They don't want anyone else to die.

Finally, we stop and we are not moved on again.

I am surrounded by others who, like me, are anxiously searching for their loved ones. Again, I start asking about my wife. Maybe now I will find her, or learn where she is. I wonder whether she might be on the other side of Deans Avenue. Perhaps she is there with some other women, and she's busy helping them? If so, she is probably trying to find me too. My wife has a mobile phone, but I do not, so she won't be able to call me. I get the idea to ask someone else to call her, but I cannot remember her number.

With every minute that ticks by without any sign of my wife, my worry grows. Questions start forcing their way into my brain. What if she is injured? Is she still inside the mosque, or near it? Did I come close to her but somehow miss her? These questions intrude upon my inner calm, and I have to fight to keep them at bay. What if she is still in danger? What if she's been kidnapped?

I am sandwiched in the unknown, stuck between good and bad possibilities. With no firm knowledge to rest upon, I lean on hope. It gives me strength. It helps me to stay calm, and to clear my mind so that I can work out what to do. *If I can't find my wife*, I tell myself, *I have to find someone who can tell me something about her.*

I come across a Somali woman, and I ask her. She is in shock and crying, but even in her grief she is kind to me. She tells me that she was in the women's room during the shooting, and that she thinks all the women and children escaped. I feel my hope flicker and briefly brighten—this could mean that Husna is safe somewhere—but then it wavers and falters. If she *is* safe, then where is she? Even if she couldn't come to me herself, she would send someone in her stead. It is not like my wife to be so silent. An uneasy feeling is taking hold, and my hope that Husna is OK is slowly being subsumed by a suspicion that something is terribly wrong. The minutes are passing, and still I have not seen her or heard anything of her. Why not?

I go to a nearby police officer and ask if he can contact his colleagues elsewhere. Can they ask around for Husna? I can see he feels for me, and he makes a few calls, but he gets no answer. 'I'm so sorry,' he says.

My heart is beating faster and faster, and I can feel anxiety pushing out what little calmness I am managing to hold on to. With some effort, I remind myself to be patient. I anchor myself in my prayers. I do my best to keep my hope alight. Hope is the best option I have.

AS THE TIME PASSES, ANOTHER concern is taking shape. I can hear my wife's voice in my head, and it is saying, *Don't forget that we have to pick up Shifa at three-fifteen today.* As promised, I have not forgotten, but I'm now not sure how I'm going to stay true to my word.

Not only am I missing Husna, who was supposed to come with me, but I also don't have my car. It is inside the police cordon, stuck where we parked it earlier today, now part of the crime scene. There is no way I'm getting my car back this afternoon, and there's no way for me to drive a normal car. And, even if I could somehow convince someone to give me a lift, my wheelchair is not collapsible, so it's too big to put in a car boot.

The thought of Shifa waiting for us to pick her up only compounds the urgency with which I seek my wife. If I can just find Husna, then we can figure out what to do. We can make a new plan together, as we always do. Perhaps we can call a wheelchair taxi so the two of us can still go to the school? Or, if that's too difficult, Husna can take a normal taxi and go on her own? There are certainly solutions, but first I have to find Husna. So I keep looking, keep asking, and time keeps on ticking by.

It ticks right on past 3.15.

In my mind, I can see Shifa waiting for us, and worrying. We always make sure that we are on time to pick up our daughter, otherwise she gets anxious. Today we are late, and I still don't know where Husna is. I have no idea when we are going to make it to Shifa's school. I realise that I have to find some way to contact the school, so that they can let Shifa know why Husna and I are not there. I'll have to phone them.

I ask a man standing beside me if I can use his phone, and he passes it to me.

'Can you help me do it?' I ask, returning it to him. Since I don't have a mobile phone, I don't even know how to use one. It is Husna who takes care of all of our phone calls.

'Of course,' he says. 'What's the number?'

'I don't know,' I reply. 'Are you able to google it?'

He finds the number for me, then passes the phone back. When I get through to the school, I'm surprised to find out it's in lockdown. They already know about the shooting.

For an instant, I am relieved: Shifa is in safe hands, and I have time to find Husna, then we can go and get our daughter together and go home. But, as quickly as it appeared, that relief evaporates, and concern takes its place. If Shifa knows about the shooting, she will be incredibly worried about us. She knew we were at mosque. Is she OK? Is she frightened? Has she been trying to get hold of us? At least she now knows I am safe. Has she called her mum?

All of these new questions take up residence in my brain with the existing questions about my wife, and my head aches with the burden of worry that it is carrying.

Then, another thought comes to join the rest: If I can't find Husna, what am I going to tell Shifa?

I AM NOT ALONE IN my anxiety, out here on Deans Avenue. In no time at all, many people have gathered and the area becomes crowded. Everywhere I look, I see worried, tear-streaked faces and tense, furrowed brows. To keep my mind from drowning in my own concerns, I turn my focus to those around me. I decide to do what I can to comfort others.

I go from one person to another. Most are people I know. 'Who are you waiting for?' I ask each of them, and they all tell me of their loved one. They are all sad, scared, anxious. Most are fighting to hold back tears, and others have them rolling down their cheeks. I do what I can to offer hope, but inevitably I hear the names of people who I have already seen dead. I cannot say anything to those who are asking for them, as I am afraid of making a mistake. I do not want to cause unnecessary grief, not when there is already so much sadness here. Instead, I hide my own sorrow and offer what comfort I can.

Through the act of comforting others, I also comfort myself. I remind myself to hope for the best. When I tell others that now is the time to be strong and positive, so that we might face whatever awaits us, I am reaffirming that advice to myself. '*Insha Allah khair*,' I say. 'By the will of Allah, something good will come out of this.'

My soothing words are not always heard, and I see that anxiety has already built a blockade in the minds of some. I can relate to how they are feeling. I sense the first stones being set in place in my own mind. My soul, too, is shaking. I am lucky not to be physically wounded, but I have certainly not escaped unscathed.

Nearby, I see some women who must have been passing by. They are embracing their Muslim sisters. Tears are streaming from their eyes. 'Our hearts are broken for you,' I can hear them saying. 'This is not Christchurch. This is not New Zealand.' Their sobs carry over the weeping, distraught crowd.

At one point, a number of Muslim women surge upon the police like a storm, begging for information.

'Please, I need to find my husband!'

'Where is my son?'

'My aunty was in there. I need to know if she's OK.'

The police are overwhelmed by the questions that roll in, one after the other, like big dark thunder clouds. 'We do not know. We're sorry,' the officers say over and over again. 'We are just doing our jobs here. We do not know anything about the crime scene. Until we hear more from the officers who are there, we have no information to give you. We're sorry.'

Their response does nothing to quell the heart-rending crying of the women surrounding them. These women are desperate, sobbing inconsolably, and their cries come from another world. They are searching for their children, their husbands, their loved ones. Some of them want to go into the mosque to see the truth for themselves, but the police will not let them. Of course the police cannot allow that—I understand that, at the same time as my own heart constricts with compassion for the women.

I do not complain. I do not show my desperation. But I feel it, lurking below like a shadow in deep, dark water. I try to keep above it, but the shadow grows and grows, threatening to pull me down. The tragic wails and cries of broken hearts are picked up by the wind and spun over our heads with the early autumn leaves, and it's as though nature is mourning with us.

The air seems to grow darker. We are enveloped in gloom. There is no salve I can apply to the agony that I am immersed in, nothing I can do to take this mortal pain away. I feel my own heart shuddering under the weight of all this hurt. It is my pain too.

A JOURNALIST APPROACHES ME, AND he asks whether I was inside the mosque. Might I be willing to speak to him? He works for a television channel, so the interview would be filmed. Ordinarily, I am a shy person. Besides a few photos that Husna has kept, I don't have pictures from the past. I am not a camera person.

But today things have changed. I feel that people need to know what has happened, so I agree to the interview. I share what I know. I am calm and I speak clearly. I say that I am sad, and that I am worried about what the future will look like. I tell the reporter that my wife is missing, that I do not know where she is. I still have no idea who is responsible for so many deaths, or why, or whether they have been caught. There is much I do not yet know.

AT LAST, I SEE SOMEONE coming towards me who I know will be able to help me find my wife. Picking her way through the crowd on Deans Avenue is Farhana, Husna's niece, and she bursts into tears as soon as she spots me. She is so relieved to find me alive.

'Where is my aunty?' she asks.

I tell her I do not know yet, that I am trying everything I can think of, but really I am just waiting and hoping.

I learn that Farhana was at work when her colleagues told her about the shooting. She immediately tried calling Husna, but when she got no answer she grew very worried. She left work and got straight into her car to drive to the mosque, but found many of the roads blocked. As she drove around and around, trying to find a way to get here, her distress burst forth in tears that she could not stem. All the while, she was also in contact with her Aunty Ayesha, Husna's sister-in-law.

When Ayesha had heard what had happened, her thoughts went immediately to Shifa. In her mind, Shifa was the priority. Ayesha figured that, if Husna and I were in trouble, our daughter would need someone to go to her. So Ayesha raced away from work and went straight to our daughter's school, planning to take Shifa somewhere safe, but she found it already in lockdown. Ayesha had also tried calling my wife, but without success.

'Aunty Ayesha is waiting at the school now,' Farhana informs me. I am so relieved to know that someone is there for our daughter.

Farhana's arrival, with her phone and its contacts list, has broken my communication barrier, and I am finally able to call some people who may know where my wife is. Farhana bolsters my flagging hope. She is very confident of Husna's skills, knowing how clever my wife is.

'My aunty will be OK,' Farhana says. 'She is definitely safe somewhere.'

I like this comment. I want it to be true.

My sole focus now is finding my wife. I want to hear her voice. I want to know that she is indeed safe.

I keep asking anyone I can for any information, anything at all. My wife is well known in the Muslim community in Christchurch, having been a part of it, like me, for over two decades. So many people know her, but no one seems to know where she is.

A few Somali women pass by, and I stop one of them and ask if she has seen Husna.

'Yes,' she replies, then explains that she saw my wife three times during the shooting. 'After that, I do not know where she went.'

I suspect there's something she's not telling me.

'Are you sure that's all you know? Is there anything else you can think of that might help?' I plead, but she shakes her head sadly.

'Husna was with the women's co-ordinator,' she tells me. 'You should call her.'

But I do not have a number for the women's co-ordinator, so I face yet another hurdle in trying to find it. I manage to get it eventually. When she answers the phone, she recognises my voice. I tell her that I need to find out what has happened to my wife.

'Yes, Husna was beside me before the shooting began,' she confirms. Her voice is shaking, but I try not to read too much into it. 'But then she went outside,' she adds, 'and I don't know what happened to her.'

My desperation is growing. I keep meeting brick walls. I need to know where Husna is. Why doesn't anyone seem to know? 'Is there someone else I can call?' I ask. 'Can you think of anyone who might be able to help me? Anywhere?'

'You could try the hospital,' she says. 'I know that injured people have been taken there.'

The black dread that has been tapping at the edges of my hope starts to break through. No one out here on the street seems to have seen Husna. If she's not out here, where is she? Has she been taken to the hospital? If so, is she injured? Is she in pain? Is she suffering? The dread curls round my heart like tendrils, sticking to each worried thought and holding fast.

Of course, there is another thought there too, one that is worse—much worse. It is hiding behind all the others, but I dodge it. I feel so helpless. The battle I have been fighting between hope and hopelessness starts to look lost. A positive outcome grows ever less likely, but I cannot bear to let my mind broach the thought of what might be the truth. That would be too painful for me, for our daughter, for so many people. I cannot think the worst. Not that. Not my lovely wife.

Then I receive a call on Farhana's phone from a man I know whose brother has been taken to the hospital. 'The hospital line is busy, so don't call there,' he tells me. Instead, he advises me to call another Muslim man who he saw volunteering in the hospital's emergency department. Perhaps he knows something?

So that's what I do. I ask if he has seen Husna. This man knows both of us very well, and has done for years, but he tells me he can't help. So many people have been brought to the hospital, he says. Can I give him any details that would help to identify Husna? He will do his best to check.

I carry on with my mission—calling, asking, praying for any snippet of information that will reunite me with my wife. I see her face in my mind, and I push away my worst fears with prayers to Allah for the best outcome. I hope against hope.

Then, Farhana brings her phone to me again.

'Someone wants to talk to you,' she says. 'I don't know who it is.'

I take her phone and I press it to my ear. 'Hello,' I say.

A low, composed voice responds, but it is smothered by the noise out here on the road. I cannot make out everything the caller is saying, but I do hear 'I have a message for you.'

My mind is racing. Who is this man? Do I know him? Why does he want to talk to me? Has he kidnapped my wife? I do my best to ignore these fears, and I listen carefully.

'Do you recognise me, Farid?' I hear. 'If you can't recognise me, I won't give you this message.'

'Can you please repeat your name?' I ask.

This time I hear it, and at last I work out who the caller is: he's a police officer. Husna and I know him very well. My heart freezes.

I know this is not good.

'My friend,' he says, 'I have bad news for you. Very bad news indeed.'

I hold myself very tight, every muscle tensed. 'Please, go ahead,' I manage to say.

'I'm afraid I have seen Husna,' he says. 'I saw her, after the shooting. I could easily identify her. I am sure it was her. I want to tell you that you should go home now. Please, do not wait out there on the road in the cold. Your wife is not coming home. She will never come home. It is going to be a very long night for you, my friend. I am so very, very sorry.'

Somehow, I summon a reply. 'Thank you for your kind information,' I say.

Then I hang up.

I return the phone to Farhana without telling her anything.

My search is over. I know where my wife is. She is with Allah.

IV

To God we belong

17.

Going home

We shall certainly test you by afflicting you with fear,
hunger, loss of properties and lives and fruits. Give glad
tidings, then, to those who remain patient, those who when
any affliction smites them, they say: 'Verily, we belong to
Allah, and it is to Him that we are destined to return.'
Upon them will be the blessings and mercy of their Lord,
and it is they who are rightly guided. (Al-Quran 2:155–7)

HOW CAN WORDS POSSIBLY DESCRIBE what it feels like to learn that your very worst fear has come to pass? How can marks on a page quantify what you experience when you discover that the thing you did not want to imagine, the thing that you fervently pushed out of your mind with hope, has nonetheless come to pass?

The answer is that they can't. Words do not have the breadth or the power to contain such immensity, or to capture such specificity. And yet, we must try. We must use the tools that we have to share what wisdom we can. We must do what we are able to show the world what love looks like, and sometimes that means trying to explain how it feels when a loved one is lost.

The pain I felt when I learned, at last, that my wife had been killed hit me like a wall of wind. The force of it threw me off balance, so that my head started to spin and I worried I might topple out of my wheelchair. If I fell, how far would I fall? Would a bottomless hole of darkness open up beneath me, a vacuum powerful enough to pull me in then keep me tumbling within it for eternity?

I held tight to the armrests of my chair, desperately trying to keep steady, while the whole world around me rocked and swayed. There was only one person who could have restored my balance, and that person was suddenly no longer there: Husna. My wife was my strongest, most steadfast support, a stable point in the turbulence, but she had been taken from me right at the moment when I needed her more desperately than ever. Where she had been just hours earlier, an emptiness now loomed, horrifying and immense, and it was consuming me.

My hope, that tentative flame which had somehow stayed alight through all of the horror and sorrow I had witnessed, burned down to one lonely ember. There it glowed then faded, fluttering on the end of a burned and blackened wick. It was barely there. I fought to fan it, to bring back even the faintest spark of brightness, but the darkness was overwhelming. It engulfed me and all of my happiness. I blinked my eyes frantically, trying to see, but it was futile. Everything was black.

My mind could not grapple with the truth. It was too big, too devastating, and even as it enveloped me I struggled against it. It pressed in on me from all sides. I felt as if the entire sky had sunk down upon me and was driving me deeper, deeper, deeper. The weight of it crushed my lungs, and as it squeezed out my breath it also stole my words. The whole world narrowed. It was terrifying.

Beneath this burden, my heart finally crumbled. It disintegrated like a desiccated husk and dispersed on the wind that had thrown my whole world off kilter. I saw the pieces of it flying away from me, fragile and dry. Gone.

I desperately fumbled for a way through the darkness, but my brain was numb. It would not respond. I felt so vulnerable in those moments. All of the awful things that I had seen since hearing that first burst of gunfire made me think more was coming. My hope died, and with it my capacity to be brave. The shock overwhelmed me so totally that I became convinced my body would give up and stop, that my own death was imminent. Everything began to move fast—too fast.

I realised I was in shock. I did not know how I was going to cope, but I knew that I had to find a way.

Somehow, in the depths of my despair, I understood that the only real source of comfort for me lay in my God Allah. I could have screamed, or cried, or wailed, but I did none of those things. Even as grief overtook me, I realised that showing my pain would only cause others to suffer more, and I did not want that. So, instead, I meditated. I applied my mental strength to calling silently for divine guidance, and I surrendered my mind to Allah. I begged for His help.

MY PLEAS WERE ANSWERED.

A verse from the Holy Quran came to me: 'As for me, patience is the most suitable [without complaint].' (12:18) These are the words of the prophet Jacob (peace be upon him), grieving for the loss of his son Joseph. They brought me peace. They were my guidance from Allah. I accepted, patiently and without complaint, that my wife was a gift from Allah, and that she had been returned to Him. *Inna lillahi wa inna ilayhi raji'un.* To God we belong and to God we shall return.

Immediately I began to feel more stable. I could see my hope begin to glimmer again, a pinprick in the darkness that cloaked me. It was slowly growing, restoring the brightness and colour to my world.

But, as my anxieties calmed, a question rose in my mind. My wife had always been there for me. After my accident, it was Husna who had cared for me. If she wasn't here, who would look after me?

I turned once again to Allah, and once again a verse from the Holy Quran came to me: 'Creator of the heavens and earth, You are my protector in this world and in the Hereafter.' (12:101) Therein lay my answer—my wife had died, but Allah will never die. I needed not worry. Allah would help me. He would take care of me, as He cares for all of His creations.

With that divine guidance, my strength returned. The world stopped rocking, and my balance was restored. My mind freed itself from the incapacitating burden of my grief and, although I was still full of sorrow, I was able to think clearly. The feeling that I was in imminent danger dissipated and, through the power of my faith, I found the courage to keep going. It was what I had to do.

Yes, my lovely wife, my other half, was gone. I would not see Husna again in this world, but that did not mean the world had ended. I was still here, still alive, and I therefore had a duty to continue the work that Husna and I had done together, even if that meant doing it alone.

I TURNED TO MY FIRST DUTY: telling Farhana what had happened to her aunty. While I had taken the call from the police officer who had seen Husna, Farhana had been watching me, but I didn't think she had guessed what we were talking about. She still believed we would find Husna. I had to tell her the truth.

For many years, as a teacher, I have taught people about patience, but this was the first time that I was truly called upon to put those teachings into practice. Summoning my inner strength, I focused on remaining composed. I did not want to break down in front of others. I wanted to be in control of my actions, to not let my circumstances control me. I did not want to offload my internal suffering on to those who were already burdened with their own woes.

I turned to Farhana, and I said calmly, 'Husna is dead.'

'No,' she said. She did not believe me. Perhaps she was suspicious of my calmness. Perhaps she simply did not want to believe what was true.

'Be patient,' I said. 'Husna is dead.'

Farhana crumpled before me, crying uncontrollably.

Within moments, people near us had noticed and were looking our way. In my desire to keep myself calm, I had forgotten that others might not be able to contain their own emotions in the same way as I tried to. I completely understood Farhana's distress, but it also pierced the fortification I had carefully built around myself. I had not wanted to make a scene. I simply wanted to leave quietly, before anyone else learned what had happened to Husna. I did not want any attention—no hugs, no condolences, no tears. I wanted to leave this street and return home, so that I could deal with my problems patiently and on my own.

But Farhana's distraught sobs made that an impossibility. The news was revealed, as Allah willed it to be. We were not meant to hide it—not from those who were gathered around us, nor from the media. My wife became the first victim confirmed to those of us waiting out there on Deans Avenue.

Now people wanted to talk to me, to hug me, to share their emotions with me. I focused on staying calm, hoping that by showing my own strength I might encourage them to also be courageous. Somehow, I managed to smile, even though it was a dry and empty expression.

'Whatever has happened has happened,' I said over and over. 'Now, we must face the challenges with courage.'

I needed to speak to Ayesha. She was still waiting outside my daughter's school. I did not want Ayesha to cry like Farhana, so I approached things differently. I had learned my lesson.

'Listen,' I said, calmly and firmly, when Ayesha answered the phone. 'You must control yourself. Husna is dead. We must be strong for my daughter.'

It was clear that Ayesha was utterly shattered, but she remained composed. 'I shall follow your guidance,' she said.

Relief washed over me. If Ayesha had broken down, I know my daughter would have done so too.

'Please do not tell Shifa anything yet,' I said. 'Just bring her home.'

I wanted to be the one to tell Shifa what had happened to her mother. It was my duty, as her loving father, to do so.

I HAD TO GO HOME, and I wanted to get there before my daughter did—but, of course, that was easier desired than done.

First, I asked a nearby police officer if there might be any chance of getting my car back. He shook his head sadly. 'No, I'm sorry.' It was part of the crime scene. It wasn't going anywhere.

So Farhana and another young man took me home. I sat in the front passenger seat, while the young man drove and Farhana sobbed in the back. It was a very difficult journey. From time to time, I said what I could to console Husna's niece. In the process, I was trying to console myself. I did not want to be silent, because I worried that silence would only exacerbate our shared pain.

As Farhana's tears flowed, I fought hard to contain my own. I wanted to cry, could feel the pressure building up inside me. All my grief was wedged in my throat, but I knew that I must keep it there. For my daughter's sake, I could not allow myself to cry, not yet. I am not a quiet or a demure crier—when I do cry, my sobs rack my whole body, and the marks of my grief remain in my reddened eyes long after the tears have dried. If Shifa saw the signs that I had been crying, it would cause her to cry too.

I also held my tears in for Farhana's sake. She was already crying a lot, and I thought that if I cried it might just increase her despair. I did not want her to exhaust herself any further—she needed to save her energy for the troubled road ahead. Many obstacles now lay before us. Things were not going to get easier from this point.

Finally, I did not cry because I wanted to keep my promise to Allah. I would be patient, and await His help and mercy. I would not complain. I knew that crying out of love would be acceptable, but even so I did not want to do that. I saw this as another test, one of the hardest imaginable, and I was determined to pass it.

ARRIVING HOME WITHOUT MY WIFE was very upsetting. Just that morning we had left together, and now I was returning alone. Husna would never come home with me again. The reality of this sank in as I wheeled myself inside our house.

Questions floated through my brain like clouds across the sky—questions that did not demand answers, questions that I did not like. They all picked and pulled at what had happened, trying to weave the truth into alternative scenarios.

Why was it me who had come home, and not Husna?

Why had I survived, while my wife had been killed?

Why was I the one fated to return to our home with a broken heart?

Would it not have been better if things had been the other way round? Shouldn't Husna have survived to care for our daughter, rather than me?

What would have happened to Shifa if we had both been killed?

I did not want to indulge these questions. They all unlocked the door to *What if . . .?* and that was a place full of pain in many forms—guilt, frustration, blame, depression, hopelessness. I did not want to go there. I knew there was no end to those questions, and they would only make me suffer more. So, I used the strength of my faith to accept what was, and in doing so let those misleading 'what if' questions pass by without acknowledgement. As the Holy Prophet (peace be upon him) said, 'If you face a loss, never say: If I did this or that [or if this or that happened], it would have been better. Rather say: Whatever was my destiny has happened. The word "if" opens the way for Satan.' (Book of Sahih Muslim)

Coming home alone, without my wife, forced me to consider the concept of *home* in a way I never had before. We use the word 'home' to mean a number of things, and we take its meaning for granted. It's so pedestrian that we don't often give it much thought. However, as I found myself waiting for my daughter in a home that had once been ours—mine and Husna's—I wondered whose home it really was. Husna had died, so did she still own it? She hadn't sold her part of it to me, and I hadn't bought it from her. Death had forced some sort of invisible transaction: it snatched away Husna's ownership of her home, by sending her to another home, but where did that leave me? Had either of us ever really 'owned' our home at all?

Many people take an enormous amount of pride in owning a home, despite the fact that no one will take their home with them when they die. Husna had not. I will not. Why do we pour so much of ourselves into a home we will never own permanently? Why do so many people spend money they do not have—money that doesn't even exist—on a place that's as impermanent as their own bodies? What, I asked myself, might the purpose *be* of owning a home in a temporary life?

The only answer I could find came from my faith: Home is, like everything else in life, a test from God. How we approach our homes shows how we approach our lives. Do we share our homes, welcome others into them? Do we make them places of love and generosity? Do we use them as places of worship, places where we pray for the peace and good of all?

We have a choice about what we do with our homes, even if we never really own them in the way we might think we do. This concept extends beyond the four walls of the house we live in, too—it stretches all the way out past the nations we call home to the planet we live on. If we want our homes to be peaceful, to be inhabited by people who love and share, that is something that starts within the houses we live our lives in.

These thoughts led me, naturally, to think about our home beyond this life. My faith tells me what that home is, and I thought about where my wife had gone, where I would go one day. When we die, we leave our home on earth behind. Someone else inherits it or buys it and it is theirs until they, too, die or sell it. It keeps changing hands long after each owner is dead and gone. Meanwhile, our true home—the home that is permanent—is the one that awaits us in the next life, and that is a home we must work hard to achieve. This reminded me of my duty here in this life: to make use of however much time remains to me to spread love, peace and harmony. For it is good work that qualifies a soul to reach their true home in Paradise.

18.

Telling Shifa

On no soul does Allah place a burden greater than it can bear. (Al-Quran 2:286)

HUSNA ALWAYS USED TO CALL me 'Softie' whenever it came to anything regarding our daughter, and she was quite right. If there's ever anything that Shifa needs, I *am* a big softie. Indeed, my heart is soft when it comes to any person—that's what enables me to be compassionate to my human brothers and sisters, but it's also the thing that causes me pain on behalf of others.

As I sat at home, waiting for Shifa to return from school, I searched desperately for a way to deliver the tragic news about her mother so that it would not cause her pain—but, of course, no such way existed. Just the thought of the words I would have to speak cut through me like a knife. As I battled with the words, I realised they were not the problem; the issue lay with the message they carried, and there was nothing I could do to change that.

The one thing I did not want to do was to burst into tears or break down in front of Shifa. I knew that would only exacerbate her grief. The task felt insurmountable—I was worried that it was more than my heart could bear, and that I might not be capable of getting the words out. So I thought of Moses (peace be upon him), seeking God's help, in the Holy Quran: 'My Lord, expand for me my breast [with assurance], and ease for me my task, and untie the knot from my tongue that they may understand my speech.' (20:25–8) Like Moses, I surrendered the task and how I would conduct it to God.

I was extremely concerned about my daughter's well-being, and had no idea how she might react to such terrible, unwanted news. I did not know if she would be able to handle such an unwelcome truth. Would she break down? How would the scars of this tragedy affect her in the long term? How would she live without her dear mother? I was painfully aware of how young my daughter was to lose her mother—and she had lost her in the worst, most sudden way imaginable. She would never have her mother hug her again, or pick her up from school, or tell her 'yes, I do love you, *pakhi*'. How could Shifa possibly cope with it all? I could not stop my mind from imagining the very worst.

Of course, the one person I desperately wanted to talk to about this was also the person whose very absence lay at the root of it all: Husna. My lovely wife was the only person with whom

I shared all of my worries, and now she was not here to help me navigate the most difficult of them. It was a truly awful time for me, and my soul was caught in a dark and terrifying struggle. At one point, I even asked myself, 'Farid, is this the end of your everything?'

But then I realised that my questions were just more 'what ifs'. All they were doing was causing me pain over something that had not even happened, which only added unnecessary weight to the burden of grief I felt for what *had* happened. So I let go of those worries. I surrendered my future to Allah, and begged Him to bestow mercy upon me and my injured heart, mercy upon my daughter. *Allahummar-hamnaa, fa-innaka ar hamurraa-hemeen.* O Allah, bestow Your mercy on us. Surely You are the best to bestow mercy.

My trust in my God Allah gave me the courage I needed. I had faith in Him, and I knew that He would help both me and Shifa. As it is said in the Holy Quran, Allah does not place a burden upon a soul that surpasses what that soul can bear. Even though this was going to be the most difficult task I had ever undertaken, I knew that Allah would give me the peace and strength I would need to do it. And what Allah would do for me in my grief, He would also do for my daughter.

SHIFA, JUST LIKE HER MOTHER, is full of smiles. She greets the world with a calmness and love that brings peace to those around her. I know my daughter's face so well—I spent many years, while she was very young, gazing down at her smile while she sat in my lap or played around my wheelchair. She has always reserved a special brightness for the moments when she spots me or Husna and her eyes connect with ours.

But I have never seen her face look the way it did when she came home that afternoon of Friday 15 March. I hope I never see it that way again. A grim shadow of anxiety had slipped over her usually pleasant expression, and every feature told of the turmoil she felt within. She was anxious—so incredibly anxious. It broke my heart.

I was waiting for her at our front door, and she rushed towards me like a storm. Normally, she waves and smiles when she sees me, but there was no room for either gesture on this day. It was as though she had no mood. She hurtled towards me, drawn by the urgent desire to hear what I had to say—Ayesha, true to her word, had not said a thing. Perhaps my daughter hoped that my words would set her fears to rest, restore her peace of mind, but it was clear that she knew something was terribly wrong. She ran to me like a child who is lost and has just found her father, but is still searching for her mother.

'Where is Mum?' she asked immediately.

'She is with Allah,' I replied without hesitation, and I put one arm round my daughter.

Shifa knew what my words meant. I did not lie, but I could not bear the blunt force of saying that Husna had been killed. That would have been too painful for both of us. Without my faith, I do not know how I ever would have had the strength to answer such a question.

Then my daughter said, 'Are you telling me that I no longer have a mother?'

'Yes.' It was all I could say. I wish I could have found smoother words, but there were none.

Shifa began to cry. I was still holding her, and I could feel the force of the grief that was contained within her. I held on to her as tightly as I could, as much for my own comfort as for hers. I knew she was struggling against the truth, didn't want to accept it.

'You must be lying,' she said.

'Your dad does not lie.'

Then, as the full force of it hit her, she in turn hit me. 'You must be lying!' she said again. 'I don't believe what you are saying! Let me go! I don't want to be here.'

She was just fifteen years old. Of course this was how she reacted. Her response was natural. I knew she needed time.

'Where will you go?' I asked.

'To my room,' she replied. She was crying, but she was not hysterical. I could feel the pain in her heart as though it were my own.

'OK,' I said. 'But, please, call me for anything that you need. And never forget that I love you.'

AS SOON AS SHIFA DISAPPEARED into her room, a steady flow of visitors into and out of our house began. Fatima, Husna's sister-in-law, arrived with her three-year-old daughter to help Ayesha and Farhana keep an eye on both me and my grieving daughter. After Fatima came others—many others. News of Husna's death had travelled fast and was deeply felt by so many who knew her—neighbours, people from her classes at mosque, people from the Muslim and Bangladeshi communities. Some arrived at our home crying. Some were afraid. Some were angry. They all had questions, and they all needed consolation.

When I had first got home, I'd been welcomed by a ringing telephone. I did not want to talk to anyone, so I ignored it.

'Why don't you answer the phone?' the young man who had driven me and Farhana home had asked.

'I am too tired,' I said. I simply wished to process my grief in private.

The phone stopped ringing . . . Then it started again.

So I gave in and answered it. It was an old friend who lived in Auckland. He was crying. I saw two options before me: either cry with him, or console him. I chose the latter, for my own sake as much as for his.

When I hung up, the young man with me was also upset.

'I haven't lost anyone close to me, but I can't bear your pain,' he said. 'How come you are not crying?'

Then he broke into tears, so I consoled him too.

'You are a strong man,' he told me. 'I wish I had your self-control.'

I knew that I was not really strong. Providing advice and consolation was my coping mechanism, and I was lucky to have it in those hours after coming home without my wife. There were many, many tears in our house that afternoon and into the night. The phone kept ringing, but I did not answer it again. There were people before me I had to talk to first.

Our neighbours came to see us, emotionally wounded and disturbed. 'We are so sorry,' they said to me over and over. 'We don't know how we can comfort you, but we are here for you if you need us.' They cried helplessly, and their pain only increased mine, but their loving gestures and compassion moved me. I consoled them so that I would not cry with them. I worried that if I started I might never stop, and that my tears would only increase theirs.

By this time, news of the attack had spread all over the world. I learned that it was not just our mosque, Masjid al-Noor, that had suffered casualties, but also Linwood Islamic Centre, just over ten minutes' drive away. The number of the dead was significant and still rising, as authorities and medics toiled to get a grasp on the full scale of the tragedy. I also discovered that police had four suspects in custody. Later in the evening, they announced that just one was connected with the shooting and had been charged with murder: a 28-year-old man from another country, who had been stopped and arrested not more than 40 minutes after police received the first call about the attacks.

One of our old neighbours who visited said to me, 'I hate that this has happened! I wish I was not white.' She was devastated at the loss of Husna, and grappling with the consequences of one man's hate.

'You must not blame yourself for someone else's wrongful actions,' I replied. 'A killer is a killer. Killing has no connection with race, skin colour, nationality or religion.'

By far the biggest crowd of mourners was the young Bangladeshi families. To them, Husna had been a mother figure. They came to our home because they did not know where else to go, what else to do. Some were still new to this country, and they were scared, sad, angry and unsure. They had so many questions, and I did my best to answer them, calm them, try to show them how to be positive even when faced with tragedy. I spent many hours counselling them, and through consoling others managed to provide some comfort to myself. At the very least, I stemmed the full flow of my grief from bursting forth.

Providing comfort to those who came to our house proved incredibly beneficial for me. When our visitors had descended upon us, I'd been forced to abandon my fear, grieving and tiredness in order to greet and talk to them. Caring for others helped me to be calmer, to be patient and to think more positively. If I'd stayed alone as I had initially wished, the evening would have only been more sorrowful and devastating for me. Our visitors were ultimately a burden that I could bear, and one that I needed.

Finally, around 11 p.m., I asked everyone to leave. I needed to spend time with my daughter. I also needed some privacy to talk with Farhana, Ayesha and Fatima. We all needed to discuss how we would navigate the difficult days and weeks to come.

IN ALL THOSE HOURS, AS I spoke to others, Shifa was my main concern. I had let her go to her room so she could have some space, but I did not want to leave her alone. Without her mother, I was all she had. She was also all I had. We needed each other. Family was our foundation and, if we did not hold on to one another, what was left of our little family might crumble.

I wanted to be with my daughter. I wanted to talk to her so that I could understand what was going through her mind. I wanted to share my grief with her, and for her to share hers with me. So I called her, and she came out of her room.

She was calm, and though she looked sad she was not crying.

My daughter's composure and strength were so impressive to me in that moment.

'*Abbee*,' she said, 'did I hit you when you gave me the news? I'm so sorry.'

Her apology gave me such joy. She had hit me only gently, and it was nothing compared with what she must have been feeling inside, but even so she had the self-awareness to remember it. Here was her loving and caring nature on full display, even in the midst of her own pain.

I also saw wisdom in her calmness. She had taken the time alone in her room to speak to her friends on the phone, to seek their help, and she had found a way to bring her painful emotions back under her control. She was no longer letting them control her.

Seeing that she was thinking more clearly, I took the opportunity to offer her some fatherly advice.

'From now, I am your mother and your father,' I said, 'and you will be my daughter and my mother. We shall change our roles to adjust our lives.'

I could not help shedding tears as I said these words. I meant every one of them.

Shifa nodded.

'You have lost your mother, but you have not lost your father,' I went on. 'You have still got me. The worst could have happened today. Both your mother and I might have died. Let us be happy with what we have.'

Shifa absorbed all of this with grace. 'I love you, *Abbee*,' she told me, and I felt my poor, shattered heart swell.

FARHANA, AYESHA, FATIMA AND HER little daughter, Fareeha, were still with us, and it was very important to me that we all talk together about Husna's death. I did not want us to pretend as though nothing had happened, to avoid looking at death for what it was. Instead, I wanted us to face it bravely, to discuss it openly. The sooner we faced our new reality, the sooner we would be able to discover the path towards recovery. I wanted us to be able to work through our grief and our emotions together so that we might turn our focus to helping others.

'This loss is a test for us,' I told Shifa and the others. 'To pass it, we need to be patient. It is a temporary loss but a permanent gain. Husna is in Paradise, and we should do good work to be reunited with her. Until we join her in Paradise, we should accept this temporary separation happily. That is what Allah loves, and He will reward us for it.'

At this, my daughter spoke up. 'I was aware that death can come at any time,' she said, 'but I did not expect Mum to die so soon. It is a hard lesson, but an important one.'

I agreed. 'Let us carry on with our normal lives, but be prepared for death.'

Next, I turned to the future. 'We have two choices,' I said. 'One is to moan and to be overcome with sadness, which will destroy us. The other option is to be strong.' I looked at my daughter. 'Which one shall we choose?' I asked her. 'I need your advice.'

Shifa considered her response carefully. 'I do not want others to see me weak. I won't let that happen,' she said. 'Although I will be sad, I will also be stronger. I want to continue my study to fulfil Mum's dream.'

Seeing my daughter handle this hardship with such wisdom and resilience gave me great relief. I felt my worries abate. She was every bit her mother's daughter. I am certain that Husna would have been just as proud as I was to see how maturely our daughter faced the most awful adversity.

We then discussed family, and what our family team looked like now. Yes, we had lost one of our team members, but that simply meant we needed to reorganise. As a team, we needed to work together with what we had, even if that was difficult. We needed to be united. I knew that one way we might succeed as a family team was to embrace positive actions, and to do so quickly. Inaction only provides space for grief to expand, while activity can offer a roadmap through sadness by keeping the mind and the body busy. So, together, we made a list of various duties, then delegated them.

Talking and planning was a balm to our pain. We were all hurting, in shock, disbelieving, but sharing our feelings helped us to remember that we were not alone. We were able to look beyond the crisis we found ourselves in and cast our gazes to the future. We used the pull of that future—tragically and irreversibly altered as it was—to keep us moving.

Right from the start, in the aching hours after the tragedy, we set in place the habit of talking. Going forward, my daughter and I in particular would need to talk to one another, so that we might continue to inspire and encourage each other to keep moving forward.

IN MY DAUGHTER'S CHALLENGE TO me the moment she learned of her mother's death lay profound wisdom. When she told me that she did not believe that she no longer had a mother, my daughter captured the essence of this tragedy. Her mother might no longer be here on this earth, but her love is. Husna's motherly love continues to do the work that Husna did while she lived: it cherishes Shifa, shelters her and inspires her to love in the way her mother did. Husna's love for Shifa will never die.

Furthermore, Husna's love lives on in the grace and comportment of her daughter. Shifa carries her mother's light and goodness within her, and continues to distribute it to those around her, just as her mother always did.

Love does not know limits. It was there with me, divine and delivered through God's mercy, when I told my daughter the news that no father ever wants to impart. It was there with my daughter when she challenged me, and when she later apologised. It came to our home, in the hours after Husna died, in the hearts and souls of those who wept for her loss and wanted to check that we were OK. It was everywhere in the responses of so many all over our city and our country after the attack in which Husna and 50 others were killed.

My wife's death was a product of a killer's hate, but her love superseded any destruction he attempted to sow. It lives on.

Love lights the way forward.

19.
Moving forward

By the glorious morning light, and by the night when
it is still, your Guardian-Lord has not forsaken you
[O Prophet], nor is He displeased. And surely the Hereafter
will be better for you than the present. And soon your
Guardian-Lord will give to you that with which you shall
be well pleased. (Al-Quran 93:1–5)

I DID NOT GO TO bed that first night without my wife until around two in the morning. I was utterly, totally exhausted. My back ached. I needed to put my feet up. All I wanted was to rest, to feel the soft touch of my bed against my sore body.

Since the day we were married, 24 years earlier, Husna and I had done everything together, including going to sleep at the end of one day and waking up the next. She was always there—except now she wasn't. In my fatigue, I became delusional. I thought I saw Husna with me in our room. Then I blinked, and she disappeared. One minute she had been there and the next she was gone. Grief stabbed at my heart. I struggled to grasp what was real and what was not, what I was seeing and what was actually before me.

Someone was helping me out of my wheelchair and into my bed. She was making sure I did not fall.

'Husna?' I said.

But of course it was not my wife. It was Farhana, Husna's niece, and when she heard me call her by her aunty's name she started to weep. Then she left me to find sleep, but my grief came for me instead.

As I lay down on my bed, I felt empty. Sorrow and loss had hollowed me out. Where my heart had been was a hole, dark and deep and terrifying. In the pit of it burned a searing pain that dried up everything inside me.

I rested my head on my pillow and turned off the light. I was alone, shrouded in the night, and Husna's absence weighed heavy and hard on my soul. I willed the tears that I had held at bay all day to come, but they eluded me. Usually, I cry easily, but all my eyes would do was burn. The tears were not there. In the heat of my pain, they had evaporated. My heart was hurting so much that it did not want to let any more pain escape, but holding my sorrow back only heightened my agony.

So, instead of crying, I lay on my bed like a log, feeling half alive and half dead. I hovered in that awful place, without peace or comfort. I wanted desperately to rest, knew my body needed it, but I simply could not.

The headache that had been with me all evening pounded at my temples. I considered taking a homeopathic remedy to ease it, but I could not summon myself to get out of bed and find it. The pain thrummed along every inch of my skull and impeded my attempts to think about the events of that terrible day. I could not think straight, and could see only one way through the dark and lonely night before me: prayer.

A verse from the Holy Quran came to me: 'And seek Allah's help with patience and prayers.' (2:153) Peace had gone from my mind, but I knew that prayer would help to restore it. So I followed that verse, and it led me to another: 'It is He who sent down peace and calmness into the hearts of the believers, that they would increase in faith.' (48:4)

As I prayed, I felt the tears well in the corners of my eyes. At last. My heart cooled, it softened, and it eased its stranglehold on my grief. Soon, I was crying like a baby, and through my sadness I felt peace returning to my soul.

In my prayer, I conversed with my Lord Allah, and He guided me out of the darkness of that night towards the dawn. He restored my sense of peace, so that I might face what waited for me with courage and serenity. Thanks be to Allah, in His mercy, for caring for me in my darkest moments.

IN THE MORNING, I FELT my wife's absence keenly. I had to remind myself that she was not on holiday, was not a telephone call away. She was gone, and she would not come back. I missed her desperately, but I also did not want missing her to bring me to a standstill. I held her in my heart, even as I readied myself to move forward without her.

Usually, our mornings progressed of their own accord, directed by our various commitments. On Saturdays, Husna and I took a Quran class for Bangladeshi adults, and on this particular Saturday Husna had also been scheduled to train some women in washing and preparing the bodies of the dead. Now, though, my wife was one of the dead awaiting that ritual.

Our schedule had been torn asunder by the tragedy of the day before. For a start, it wasn't our schedule anymore; it was mine, and mine alone. Without a set of predictable tasks to follow, I felt cast adrift on a new and terrible ocean. I would have to face the day alone, without Husna alongside me at the helm of our boat. As I lay in bed, I started to cry again. I was in no hurry to get up and face such an open-ended day.

But, thankfully, through my prayer, I had been able to restore the clarity of my thoughts. So, even though I was reluctant to get up, I was already working out where I should begin. First, I needed to find out where Husna was—should I call the hospital? Perhaps they would be able to tell me where my wife's body was, and when she would be released. Then I needed to begin organising her funeral. In our years in Christchurch, Husna and I had helped to organise many funerals for our Muslim brothers and sisters, so I knew the procedure well. Just eight months earlier, in fact, Husna and I had helped to organise the funeral for her older brother and Fatima's husband, Kauser Ahmed, who died from leukaemia. He was only in his mid-forties, and left behind his beloved wife and three-year-old daughter, both of whom Husna and I had taken into our care.

Islamic teaching calls for the body of a Muslim to be buried as soon as possible after death. The burial is preceded by bathing and shrouding, then the Janazah prayer. Our belief is that a quick burial is rewarding, so when a loved one dies we do everything we can to expedite the process.

Here in New Zealand, however, there are a few additional steps that aren't part of proceedings in Muslim-majority countries—we also need to obtain a death certificate and arrange a burial plot. Both these steps add time to organising a burial. How long it takes to get the death certificate depends on the cause of death, and it's only once we have the death certificate that we can contact the city council about organising the burial plot; we hand over the money for the plot, and then the council tells us how many hours we have to wait before the grave will be ready. Then, in those hours, we take care of the rites of washing and wrapping.

At the funeral, the community comes together to pray for the deceased, and the Janazah prayer is led by an imam, then the burial takes place. Whoever is able to accompanies the deceased in their journey to the grave—we believe that helping in burial is a good deed, and Allah rewards the helpers. As a result, anyone can join in with the burial, no matter whether or not they are from the same family, community or faith. It is a rite that transcends our differences, that brings us together.

Bearing all this in mind, I felt the pressure of time. I needed to start arranging my wife's funeral as soon as I could, but the tragic circumstances of her death erected a barrier before I had even begun. Until her body was released, there was nothing that I could do. I did not know whether I should call the hospital, or whether I should wait to be called. I already knew from the scenes I had witnessed at Masjid al-Noor that there would be many, many deaths for the authorities to process, and that must only slow things down.

EVER SINCE I HAD COME home the previous day, the phone had been ringing. It rang all through the evening, into the night, and kept ringing until the new day arrived. After talking to my friend in Auckland, I had simply let it ring, figuring that those who had words to share could leave a message. However, it seemed that many people just kept ringing and ringing without leaving a message. They wanted to hear my voice, and failed to realise that their insistence only caused me more stress. I did not have the emotional capacity to talk to all of them, not just yet.

As I lay in bed trying to work out how to begin my day, the phone rang yet again, and this time I decided I'd answer it. I was feeling more capable of doing so than I had the day before.

But I soon realised I was better to leave it to its ringing. The callers answered me with tears, and that just served to bring my own grief bubbling up to the surface. They wanted to talk about my wife, about how good she was, how much she had helped them, how grateful they were to her, but I could not deal with so many memories all at once. I knew the callers were only trying to show me their love, but their tears threatened to dissolve the calm my night-time prayers had restored.

I felt myself growing exhausted. I am just one man. I only have so much energy, and I needed what little I had for the tasks before me. I'd spent the previous evening consoling and listening; today was for action. Right now, I needed positivity, not more negativity. That was what would help me to be strong, to be brave. Crying and blaming would only bring me to a halt, and every minute was crucial. All my life I have been more of a doer than a wailer, and this morning was no different.

So I stopped taking calls. I handed that task to Farhana, and told her to bring me only the urgent and most important ones. I turned my focus to the funeral, to what needed to happen so that we could bury Husna.

There was one useful thing that came from the few calls I did take: they told me how far the ripples of this tragedy had already spread. I began to realise that wounds had been inflicted not just on those of us who had been there in al-Noor and Linwood mosques, on those of us who had survived and who had lost our loved ones. The hateful attack on our community had harmed our whole city, our whole country. Our home had been attacked, and it was grieving. Everyone was weeping.

People who had not even been there had nonetheless become victims. They could not move beyond their helplessness and disbelief to find a way to hope. They had lost sight of the future, and they needed someone to give them a positive jump-start. It was their negativity that inspired me to respond with positivity.

Just as I had two decades earlier, when that drunk driver hit me with his car, I resolved not to become a victim twice over. The man who, just the day before, had killed my wife and so many others had already made me a victim to his actions; I would not let myself become a victim to despair as well. I would not grant his hateful attack my own fear. Instead, I would show love.

In her life, my wife showed love to so many. That love was coming back to me now in the grief of those who had felt her love, and although their sorrow caused me pain it also reinforced the message that Husna had lived by: love begets love.

I promised I would do whatever I could to spread a message of hope and positivity. Doing so became my new mission after the loss of my lovely wife.

BEFORE LONG, FARHANA BROUGHT ME the phone. On the line was a young Bangladeshi man named Belayet Hossain. He and his wife had been very fond of Husna—my wife had helped his when she gave birth to their baby boy. They were distraught to hear of Husna's death, and he was calling me from the hospital, where he was frantically searching for friends who had been in the mosque during the attack.

'An emergency help centre has been set up at Hagley College,' he told me. 'It's there to give support to victims and their families. The police are giving updates about what is happening with the injured, and with the bodies of the dead.'

I thanked him sincerely. 'I will be there soon,' I said.

That call was very important to me. It shed some light on the path ahead. At last I had some information that would help me to get started with organising my wife's funeral.

Next, I had to get myself down to Hagley College. Earlier, a woman called Donna McAleer, who was one of Husna's colleagues and friends, had called to offer her condolences. Donna had worked with Husna caring for vulnerable people in our community, and she was very distressed about Husna's death—she wept on the phone, but she wanted to turn her sorrow into action. In fact, she had been extremely insistent about helping me and Shifa—she'd wanted to come right over to our house. I'd had to be equally insistent to stop her.

'I will call you when I need your help,' I had assured her.

Now I had a task for Donna.

I called her back. 'I need to get to Hagley College,' I explained. 'Would you be able to drive me there?'

'Gary and I will be right over,' Donna said.

And, true to her word, she and her partner arrived soon after. I greeted them with a smile even though I felt I might burst into tears at any moment.

WHEN WE ARRIVED AT THE help centre, we were greeted with a scene unlike anything any of us could have ever imagined seeing here in our home city. There were police officers everywhere, and they were carrying guns. Seeing this, I realised the seriousness of the tragedy—and that, importantly, our country was taking it seriously. I hid the tears that my feelings of gratitude to my home and my fellow Kiwis provoked in that moment.

The carpark was packed to bursting, and we drove round and round in search of a convenient park for me in my wheelchair, but none appeared. Weaving in among the police and throngs of people, we spotted some volunteers. We pulled up alongside them and asked if they might be able to find us a park, and they soon did. There were so many volunteers, and they were all busy going from one place to another. I recognised some of them from my own community, but there were many others who had come from all across New Zealand.

When we entered the help centre, we saw just how crowded it was inside. It was as though every Muslim who lived in Christchurch—and more—had crammed into the one building. They were all hoping for news about their missing loved ones, and I soon realised that some had been here all night, waiting and praying. There were still many people who did not know if their loved ones were alive or dead. They were desperate to find out, and their exhaustion and worry showed on their faces. It was truly heartbreaking.

There were also many non-Muslim Kiwis there, offering what support they could—food, comfort, sympathy. The whole thing was overwhelming. I could not fathom how such a comprehensive and wonderful facility had been set up so quickly. Once again I felt the tears pricking at my eyes, but I determined to keep my smile on show for those around me.

As soon as those who knew me spotted me, they came to me. They all had questions that I could not answer.

'Brother Farid, you were there. Tell me, did you see my father?'

'Brother Farid, was my son in there? Was he alive or dead?'

'You went back into the mosque afterwards, Brother Farid! I do not know where my husband is. Did you see him?'

I desperately wished I could have given answers, but I could not. All I could do was advise every person who came to me to wait for word from the police or the hospital. What else could I say? I wish that I never had to face such questions in the first place, and that no one ever had to ask them of me. Their crying filled my heart with agony. I wanted to cry too. Instead, I tried to share with them the courage I knew they would need.

'Be patient,' I said. 'This is awful, but it is not the end of the world.' I moved from table to table, talking with as many worried family members as I could. They all knew that my wife had been killed, and they knew I was in pain like them. They saw that I was travelling the same road of suffering as they were, and they wanted to hear my advice. I saw in them anger, sadness, frustration and hopelessness, so I offered them Islamic knowledge for combatting and overcoming such emotions. True to my promise that morning, I spread the message of hope and positivity to as many as I could.

While I was there, the police gave a couple of briefings. Their central message remained the same: everyone was working as fast as they could to identify and return our dead to us, but because of the nature of their deaths there was an enormous amount of work involved. Our dead were part of a crime scene, and the authorities had to follow due process to ensure that everything was conducted carefully and correctly, but that would take time. I took these briefings as gentle reminders to go home and be patient. There were, of course, families who wanted more precise timing; they were grieving and scared, and understandably they wanted more certainty, even though none could be provided.

While I was there, Prime Minister Jacinda Ardern visited and spoke to us. She reiterated what the authorities had said: everything was being done to ensure that our loved ones were treated with respect and were returned to us as quickly as possible. In those early hours after the tragedy, she took the time to be with us in our grief, to acknowledge our loss. The people of Christchurch needed that from her. Our country needed it. Her actions provided a positive example for the rest of us.

Not long after I had arrived, so had some Muslim leaders and Islamic scholars. They began a programme of talks aimed at advising and calming the anxious crowds, emceed by the president of the Federation of Islamic Associations of New Zealand (FIANZ), Dr Mustafa Farouk. These speakers offered messages of positivity: be patient, be peaceful, be positive, be compassionate. They reminded those gathered to put their trust in Allah, and to be grateful for the outpouring of support they were receiving from fellow Kiwis. These speeches strengthened my hope, and reinforced my own mission to spread love.

Much to my surprise, Dr Farouk called upon me to give a talk about how I was coping so calmly, having lost my wife. It was an honour to speak to the grieving families, and I saw it as an opportunity from Allah to share my positive message.

First, I explained that I saw my wife as a gift from God, and He had seen fit to take her back, so I preferred to thank Him for the gift He had bestowed rather than complain at having it taken away. Since my wife had never been mine, I accepted her return happily. She was in Paradise, a place of happiness, and I was grateful for that. Finally, I explained the choice I had made: instead of destroying myself with negativity, I had chosen to move myself forward with positivity.

I spoke from my heart, and I believe my words were well received. I was humbled by the kind comments afterwards from those who had been listening—their feedback was invaluable, because it gave me the motivation I needed to continue to spread my message of love and hope. Little did I know, that talk would only be the beginning. From there, my message reached further and further. I had no idea just how far it would go.

I AM, BY NATURE, A shy and sensitive person, always careful about what I say. I do not like having harsh words directed my way, nor do I like directing them at others. Always at the forefront of my mind is the desire to keep my speech kind. I do not want to hurt others with my words. That's why I'm careful—sometimes too careful, perhaps—about what I say.

Despite my shyness, however, I have made an effort since I was young to learn how to speak well to a crowd. My reasoning for this is simple: one good speech can inspire many in a short space of time. Being an effective and compelling public speaker is a useful skill if you wish to inspire good in the world, and if you wish that good to go far.

For some reason, when I was still at primary school, I had this strange notion that I should be able to deliver speeches in English. It was a strong enough desire that it drove me in my studies, and I memorised every word in my English textbook. When I moved on to high school, my Bengali teacher further encouraged me by lining me up to speak at any and every function our school organised. The biggest audience I addressed comprised 10,000 people—the education minister had paid us a visit. My Arabic teacher also nurtured me as a speaker on Islamic issues. I remember these teachers with a grateful heart, and I pray for them.

Public speaking has not always come to me naturally, however, and my early attempts to master it were fraught with embarrassments. Once, when I was a first-year engineering student at Sylhet Polytechnic Institute, I volunteered to speak on behalf of my peers at a feast organised by our hostel's student union—but I did so terribly that my classmates were furious with me. They thought I'd embarrassed them too. 'Do not take the stage again,' they warned me. I heard what they were saying, but I thought, *I'll show you guys. Just give me some time.* I worked harder than ever, practising my speech on the roof of our hostel while all the other students slept. After six months, I'd improved so much that my popularity as a speaker won me the top job at the student union.

In my life beyond my student days I went on to speak in all sorts of capacities—as a teacher, giving sermons, at public gatherings, and as a marriage celebrant. But, although I was comfortable speaking to gathered crowds, I was never keen on being on camera. As I've said, I am not a camera person—but Husna's death, and the attack on our mosque, changed that. So, when I was again approached by media at the Hagley help centre, I agreed to talk to them.

Some people who heard that journalists were asking for me jokingly said, 'Oh, you are famous now! You're on the TV!'

This comment made me uncomfortable. It suggested I might be speaking for personal gain, but my motivation was quite the opposite. I still did not relish being on camera, but I did want to share my message of love and hope. I saw the media as a vehicle for fulfilling my mission to spread positivity in response to horror. In the midst of the crisis that had enveloped us, I felt I had no other choice. People needed to hear words of love, forgiveness, peace and harmony. Just as love begets love, so does hate beget hate. I wanted to do whatever I could to ensure that love triumphed.

20.
Waiting, waiting

Allah is with those who maintain patience.
(Al-Quran 2:153)

I WENT HOME FROM THE help centre at Hagley College and I waited.

I waited, I waited, I waited.

One day turned into another, while I waited to hear that Husna's body would be released to us so that we could finally bury her. I held fast to my faith in order to remain patient. I filled my time with caring for my daughter, sitting with visitors, speaking to relatives overseas and doing what I could to help various agencies and community groups. Four days later, on Tuesday, I got my car back—a huge relief, as it restored my freedom to drive myself around. And, of course, I spoke to the media. Every day, I talked to them, and my message remained the same: love, peace, forgiveness.

Although I kept myself busy, I was not used to waiting so long. It is not our custom to wait before a funeral, and I had never waited such a long time to bury a loved one. In the end, the wait stretched to a full week, and each of those days brought all sorts of difficult emotions. It was a strange, painful time, during which I fluctuated between extremes. I felt so far away from my wife, at the same time as being acutely aware that her body remained so near. I kept thinking of her lying in the hospital morgue, just thirty minutes' drive from our home. I had not seen her since that morning when we had headed to Masjid al-Noor together, so I felt incredibly detached from her. At the same time, the fact we had not been able to bury her yet—the ultimate act of detachment—kept me feeling emotionally attached to her, and I had to remind myself every day that she had died. It was like learning the news afresh, over and over and over.

In those days, I was frequently blindsided by guilt. Was I really doing enough to ensure the quickest possible burial for my beloved wife? It was my duty to do so, and I knew that Allah would question me if I neglected that duty in any way. The longer I had to wait, the more I wondered if there was something else I should be doing, some way I could speed things up—but, of course, there was nothing more I could have done. I tried to console myself that I was doing everything in my power. The most we can do is our very best, and that was certainly what I was doing.

As I have mentioned, Muslims try to have the burial completed within 24 hours of our loved ones passing away. One reason this is a good idea is that planning a funeral is very painful. It brings your loss into stark relief, reminds you of all you have to cry about. My daughter and I, and our family, had to plan Husna's funeral over and over. Each day, we had to review the funeral plan to take into account any changes or updates, and each day was a fresh wound to us. We simply wanted to bury our beloved Husna, but there was nothing we could do to make that happen any faster. There was nothing we could do but wait.

I understood that everyone involved was doing their very best to release the bodies of the dead to families as quickly as possible. I was grateful to them for their efforts. They had done their jobs in the most dire of circumstances, and I can only imagine what it must have cost them to do so. Nonetheless, I still felt sad about having to wait so long. I am, above all, a loving husband and I am guided by compassion. I simply wanted what was best for everyone, but it's difficult to find what is best in a situation so full of woe.

AT LONG LAST, ON THURSDAY, my wife's body was released from the hospital and sent to a nearby funeral home. We would perform the washing the same day, and we were offered two options: female relatives could wash my wife, as per the usual custom, or we could choose to have some Muslim female volunteers wash her instead. The latter option was offered out of concern for our well-being. My wife's death had not been a natural one, and the wound that killed her was not natural. As well as caring for my wife's body, the volunteers were caring for us; if we did not feel we were up to witnessing exactly what had happened to Husna, or if we felt it might traumatise us, the option was there to let someone else wash her body on our behalf. In the days after the attack, many Muslim men and women, led by a team of Muslim physicians, gave their time to help grieving families in this way; without their generosity, it would have been enormously difficult to get everything done smoothly. May Allah bless them.

Some families, in spite of the trauma, still preferred to wash their loved ones themselves. The professionals were careful to explain to everyone involved precisely what this meant, and what we would see. Each family chose the option that was best for them.

What did we choose? After meeting as a family—me, my daughter, Husna's two nieces and two sisters-in-law—we decided that we would wash Husna ourselves. Four women were chosen to wash her, two of whom had been trained in the process by Husna herself. I would not be part of the washing, in case I became too emotional, but I would not be jobless: my role would be to write down the procedure, step by step, to make the task easier for the women performing it. I would also be nearby, behind the door in another room, so they could ask any questions that might arise. I also hoped my proximity might give them courage.

Shifa would not be part of the washing team either, for the simple reason that I wished to save her from that pain. She was only fifteen, and the deceased was her own dear mother. She and I arrived at this decision together—as always, I asked for her thoughts before deciding the plan.

WHEN WE ARRIVED AT THE funeral home, we were greeted by a Muslim doctor who was overseeing everything. He hugged me, then guided me towards two more Muslim doctors. We spoke as he walked alongside me, but we avoided one another's eyes. I had already seen the pain in them, and it reflected my own. It was as though we had made a silent pact not to look at each other for more than an instant, otherwise all that shared pain would come out in tears. We were both there to do a job, and we focused on our separate tasks to keep the sorrow at bay.

The two other doctors assisted us with some paperwork. They were a married couple, and I could see that they were also hurting. The suffering reached so far. It rubbed off on anyone and everyone who came near it. We discussed our plans with these doctors, and made a slight amendment, at their suggestion—a female doctor would also form part of our washing team, in case any medical stitching was required on my wife's wounds.

We were then directed down a hallway towards the washing room. With every inch closer that we drew, I felt the pressure building on my faltering heart. I was trying to stay cheerful for the sake of everyone else, but I just wanted to cry. I could feel the tears welling, and with them came fear—the fear that, if the professionals with me and my team saw any of us was upset, they might take over the washing. We might not get to wash my wife's body ourselves. So I began mentally reciting verses from the Holy Quran to keep my mind busy. I prayed to Allah, asking Him to grant me and my family the strength we would need to perform the task at hand.

When we reached the door to the washing room, we were met by an incredible scene: outside, wearing aprons and prepared with gloves, stood many women. They were my wife's friends, her students, and they were joined by Muslim ladies volunteering from other parts of New Zealand. Some of these women had been meant to attend the washing lesson that Husna was never able to run on Saturday 16 March. They were all there to honour my wife, to show their respect for the woman who had shown them so much love, by washing her body before burial.

I was overwhelmed to see such a demonstration of love for my wife—but there was no way that so many women would fit in the washing room at once, so I simply said, 'May Allah grant you honour and reward for your presence here.' Then I explained that, as planned, the four chosen family members and the doctor would go in to wash my wife. The rest of us would wait outside, so that if the washing team required assistance they'd need only ask.

IT TAKES TIME TO WASH a dead body. It is not an easy task. There are particular steps to follow, and performing them correctly requires care and patience. For me, sitting outside the room where my wife's body was being washed, that meant more waiting.

As I waited, my emotions came over me like waves in the sea. They would swell and rise, then crash over me so that I was disoriented and flailing about, then I'd be granted a moment's respite as they eased and retracted—only to build up more force for the next wave.

It was all I could do not to cry. I struggled against the urge to weep, as I knew that doing so would only cause everyone around me to break down too. The area outside the washing room would descend into a place of hopeless mourning, and I did not want that. I did not think I could deal with that.

I searched for something, anything, to keep my mind busy and my emotions under control. I wanted to use the time while I waited wisely, to put it to use by giving my wife a gift. Giving can continue even after death, according to our faith. I decided to make *du'a* for Husna, then I began to recite aloud from the Holy Quran. My recitation was a celebration of all that my wife and I held dear— our marriage and our life together, the classes she and I had run together at mosque, her generosity and her faith. Husna had always been my best listener, and even in death I know she heard me. It is our belief that, although our bodies die, our souls live forever. I felt my wife's soul with me there, knew that she was all around me, and that she was listening to my Quran recitation as attentively as she ever had.

While I was reciting from chapter 92 *Al-Layl* (The Night), I stumbled on verses five and six—'So he who gives [in charity] and fears [the judgement of Allah], and [in all sincerity] accepts [the truth] and follows the best.' At the word *husna*—the best—I burst into tears. All around me, others began to cry too, the tears appearing on the cheeks of first one woman and then another.

I stopped and apologised, but the crowd was not worried. They understood. 'Do not apologise,' they said to me.

I began my recitation again, and I continued it until the washing of my wife's body was complete.

MY WAIT WAS OVER. IT was time to say goodbye to my wife.

The washing team had clothed my wife and put her in the casket, as I had requested. Then, they brought the casket to me. As they carried her to me, I continued my recitation. My heart was fluttering in my chest and I worried that it might stop altogether. I used the words of the Holy Quran to bolster my courage, as I felt all of my love for my wife, all of my memories of her suddenly crowding in on me.

I was so afraid that I might not cope with seeing her, but I knew that I had to. This was my last chance to see her, to talk to her while her soul was listening. It was also the first time I had seen her since parting ways with her the Friday before at mosque. Who could have known that this was how we would reunite? One of us alive, and the other gone.

I made my *du'a* as she lay before me. She and I had always been a team, and I wanted to preserve our unity even as I bid her farewell. I was filled with sorrow, but I wanted to give my wife happiness, so I held back my tears with the power of my words.

When, at last, I stopped reciting, I turned to the people gathered with me. We shared our love for Husna and our sadness at her loss.

'Please, join me in *du'a*, if you wish,' I said.

Du'a is a prayer of supplication or appeal, and is a heartfelt act of worship in Islam. As I made my *du'a* in Arabic, I finally let the tears I had been holding back break free. I cried a lot. It is good to cry during *du'a*, as it is a prayer that comes from the deepest part of the heart, a plea of the most profound sincerity. *Du'a* knocks at the door of Allah's mercy. For me, crying when I make *du'a* heals my pain, so that afterwards I feel refreshed and unburdened. As I prayed for my wife, I felt my tears relieving all of the weight that had been compressing my heart. Everyone around me cried with me.

I appealed to Allah to forgive my wife and to embrace her with

His mercy. I prayed to Him to accept her as His honourable guest, to keep her in peace and comfort, to connect her grave with Paradise until resurrection. I asked Him to admit her soul to Paradise, and to save her from any suffering.

When I was finished, I approached my wife's casket. I wheeled my chair as close as I could, and then I spoke to her.

'Husna, *assalamu alaikum*,' I said. 'Husna, do not worry. We are a team, and we will be a team again in Paradise, *Insha Allah*.'

I promised to carry on the good work we had done together.

'I am sure that you are smiling,' I said. 'I do not want to cry for your smile, but I will cry for the love of you. I am leaving you in the mercy of Allah. He is our guardian and He will look after you.'

I looked at my lovely wife. I knew I was speaking to her for the last time on this earth, and that knowledge filled me with unbearable pain. I would never wish such pain upon any person, not even my worst enemy. I worried I might cave under the strain of it, but I did not. I said goodbye.

'I will always love you,' I told my wife.

21.
The following Friday

Do not say about those who are killed in the service of Allah
[in the worship of Allah], that they are dead, but know they
are living. Their soul is alive. But you do not perceive it.
(Al-Quran 2:154)

SINCE SO MANY PEOPLE WERE killed in the attacks on
al-Noor and Linwood mosques, there was an enormous amount of
work for the Muslim volunteers helping to organise the funerals
and burials. The specific wishes of each and every family had to

be taken into account, and once again that all took time. Some grieving families who were from other countries wanted their loved ones returned home for burial. I knew of more than one victim whose mother was overseas and wanted her child returned to her, so that she could touch them, kiss them one last time, and say goodbye. In those instances, the bodies were washed and shrouded, then a funeral prayer was said for them before they were sent home, where another funeral prayer would be said and they would finally be laid to rest.

Other families wanted to bury their loved one on their own, in a dedicated funeral service. These families took responsibility for preparing their loved one and arranging the funeral.

There was one other option, and that was to bury loved ones as part of a mass funeral. The majority of victims' families, including ours, chose this option. Individual funerals ran back to back all throughout Thursday, and the mass funeral was set for Friday, following a public Jumu'ah in Hagley Park. My wife would be farewelled along with more than two dozen other people whose lives had been taken from them just one week earlier. Mourners would be given time to spend with their loved one, then one funeral prayer would be said for all the deceased, who would then be buried one by one by their relatives.

Perhaps you are wondering why we chose the mass funeral for Husna. It was a decision I considered carefully, and consulted my family about, and there were a number of reasons it felt right for us. As I've said, I have never believed Husna was mine; she was a gift from God not just to me, but to everyone whose life she touched. My wife mattered to so many people, and there were many who wished to farewell her. She was an integral part of our community, of our city, of this country, and I felt it was only fitting that she should be laid to rest at a funeral that was open to one and all, no matter what walk of life they came from. She opened her life to others, so it made sense for her death to be open to them too.

To me, a mass funeral was also an apt response to what had been a mass killing. I liked the idea of people coming together to share in their grief and prayers. Such a gathering would be a symbol of unity, and a powerful one at that. It sat in direct contrast to the impulse that had driven the killer to take the lives of those who were to be buried. He sought to reap fear and separation; we would respond with love and togetherness, even while we grieved. There is no act of hate that will ever sunder the strength of unity, try as it might. We would do as our loved ones had been doing the Friday before, and unite in prayer and peacefulness. We would open our arms to any who wanted to join us.

I also knew the gathered crowd would be a big one. A prayer shared by so many would be incredibly significant. As Muslims, we believe that the more attendees there are at a funeral, the better it is for the deceased. More people means more prayers to Allah requesting His mercy for the deceased. I wanted the best for my wife, who had always wanted the best for others, and I could do no better than having the hearts and minds of many praying for her, and for those who had died with her, all at once.

There was also the simple fact that the mass funeral relieved me of much of the distress around planning it. There were so many kind volunteers who gave their time to help with the organising, and to ensure that we were well taken care of. Letting them show their love through their actions was a way for me to show my gratitude for their efforts. The mass funeral would also be easier on them—it gave them one event to attend and offer their prayers, when their precious time was already so stretched because of their generosity towards us. Many had been working day and night, so it would not have been practical for them to attend every single individual funeral, but I knew they would want to pay their respects and offer their prayers—and, indeed, given their own grief and trauma, that they would need to do so.

I GOT UP EARLY ON the morning of Friday 22 March, already tired from lack of sleep. I had spent the night alternating between worrying about the funeral and crying. I was particularly concerned about my daughter. Shifa still had not seen her mother's body; today she would, and she would also be saying goodbye to her. Thinking of this constricted my heart. I wished that I could spare my daughter from the pain I knew that she would feel, but I knew there was no other way but forward. We had to meet the challenges ahead, and we would do it together.

Even though I was not hungry, I forced myself to eat some breakfast—half a piece of toast and some boiled egg. I couldn't finish it, but it was something, at least.

While I was eating, a relative, Ferdous Alam, arrived at my house with a friend of his who had come over from Australia. They were there to accompany me to a funeral home, where I had promised to lead the funeral prayers for three young Bangladeshi men who had been killed. I had known each of these men—they had attended my Saturday classes at mosque. Afterwards, I would head to Jumu'ah at Hagley Park, then to my wife's funeral.

I drove to the funeral home with Ferdous and his friend, and despite knowing the way I somehow managed to get lost twice. My guests did not suspect a thing—I was driving carefully, and making an effort to talk to them so that they would not think that I was unsettled. To them, I must have seemed composed, but my brain felt like it was running at a delay. I was struggling to keep up with each moment, to keep moving forward, as my emotions weighed me down and left my mind sluggish, causing me to make mistakes.

We eventually arrived at the funeral home, and were greeted by the smiles of people we knew. I smiled back at them, our shared effort serving to comfort one another. I was told that one of the deceased was in the casket and ready for his funeral prayer, and I was led to him. Two imams—one from Auckland, and the other from Australia—helped me to perform each of the three Janazah prayers, then I led the *du'a* at each family's request.

In attendance at the final prayer was the young man's widow, still deadened by her own grief. She was weak, exhausted, broken, and some community members requested that I speak to her; they hoped that, since I too was grieving the loss of my spouse, I might be able to offer some solace. I spent some time sitting with her, trying to help her to find her capacity for hope and courage, but she had been flattened by her husband's tragic death. She was young, as was he. I saw her pain, felt it as my own, but also saw how heavy her burden was, given her youth.

Being so close to the widow's pain exacerbated my own, especially having just prayed for three dead men. It was incredibly draining for me to be exposed to so much grief before I had even turned my focus to my own wife's funeral, but I did it because it had to be done. It was an honour to be asked, and I had to do what I could. Each of these men had grieving relatives far away who were depending on us, here in New Zealand, to care for their loved ones in their absence. We all had to do our best.

AFTER THOSE MORNING FUNERAL PRAYERS, I had to race to get to Hagley Park in time for Jumu'ah. I was already exhausted —I had never performed so many funeral prayers in one day, and today had barely begun. When I arrived at Hagley Park, my emotional pain was joined by physical pain, as my wheelchair jerked over the bumpy ground. The going was tough, and my slow progress was made slower by the many who wanted to stop and talk to me.

But my physical difficulty upon arrival was offset by the joy I felt on that occasion. A week earlier, my prayers and those of my fellow worshippers had been ripped through by bullets. Today, in a show of solidarity that transcended any of our perceived differences, people from all over the city—indeed, from all over the country and even further afield—had come together in love and hope. Thousands of people had gathered to show that we were one country, and one people. It was very moving.

Prime Minister Ardern opened proceedings. 'When any part of the body suffers, the whole body feels pain,' she said to the assembled crowd. 'New Zealand mourns with you. We are one.'

Her words that day and in the days to come echoed not only around Hagley Park, but around the world. Her message of love and compassion found a home in the hearts of people near and far.

At 1.30 p.m. *azan* sounded. It was followed by two minutes of silence in remembrance of those who had died—a silence observed at the same time by Kiwis all over the country.

Then Jumu'ah began with Imam Gamal Fouda's sermon. He had been there with us at Masjid al-Noor and had survived. He delivered a powerful message of love and peace to the thousands gathered. He spoke of the glorious status of those who had been killed, who were martyrs in the sight of Allah. He called for those who had survived, those who had lost their loved ones, to be patient. He encouraged us all to be strong, and reminded the country that even in heartbreak we were not broken. He offered his sincere thanks to those first responders who had put their own lives at risk to protect their Muslim brothers and sisters, and gave thanks to New Zealand for showing love, not hate.

The imam's sermon was followed by a prayer, during which all Muslim men and women lined up alongside one another. Muslims pray in a straight line, as the angels pray to Allah; we do as the angels do to show sincerity, humility and discipline. Side by side, we faced the same direction, praying as one. In prayer, each worshipper demonstrated his or her humility by bending down and prostrating before Allah, Almighty God.

New Zealand is a peaceful country, and Jumu'ah that Friday was a mass demonstration of our peacefulness. Kiwis of every description—rich and poor, powerful and lowly, old and young, religious and secular—came together in shared love and sadness for their human brothers and sisters. Together, we showed the rest of the world what a truly peaceful gathering looks like, and the world was watching. The world saw us.

ON THIS FRIDAY, FULL OF grief as it was, I found more than one opportunity for joy. Here, joy co-existed with tragedy; the two were so closely interwoven that it was impossible to extract one from the other.

Joy lay in my presence there at Hagley Park. I was alive, and it was thanks to the grace and mercy of Allah. He had granted me more time here on this earth, so that I might continue my good work and so that I might pray for my dear wife.

Joy lay in my reunion with two men who had been with me at Masjid al-Noor the Friday before, and who I had not seen since. They had both been injured, and one of them had lost his son, a wonderful young man who left behind a wife and little baby. They met my tears with their own, and we shared in our grief.

Joy lay in seeing so many people who knew me, and who loved my wife. They had come from all over the country, and some from overseas, to offer their condolences and their support.

After the prayer had ended, a journalist approached me.

'Mr Ahmed,' he asked, 'how do you feel today compared with what you went through last Friday?'

I answered from my heart. 'Last Friday, I cried with sadness. This Friday, I cried with joy.'

BY THE TIME THAT I made it back to the car after Jumu'ah, I was running late. I had been delayed talking to people; just like my wife, I have never been very good at saying no. I found Shifa and Farhana already in the car, anxiously waiting for me. It was past time for us to leave for the cemetery, where we would perform our final task for the day: burying Husna.

Once we were on the road, the gridlocked traffic and the red lights delayed us further. I was doing my best to get us there as fast as I could but, just as I had that morning, I found myself losing my way, which only served to steal more precious minutes. Then, when we finally arrived at the cemetery, we could not find a park nearby, and I was forced to park on a grassy area some distance away. For the second time that day, I had to push myself across bumpy earth not made for a wheelchair, and what little energy I had left was sorely depleted by the time we arrived at the cemetery gates.

Many people were milling about outside, but some volunteers were waiting for me and Shifa. They guided us in with the other family members; everyone else had to remain outside, due to space. We entered a large tent where the bodies of our loved ones lay, waiting for the mass funeral prayer. The caskets were all lined up, one alongside the other.

One of the volunteers handed us a number.

'This is the number of your wife's casket,' the volunteer explained. 'I'm sorry, you won't be able to spend much time with her, as the prayer is about to start.'

Shifa and I found Husna easily. Many others were already alongside her. With me and my daughter were Husna's brother-in-law, her two sisters-in-law, and her two nieces. And there were others who came to pay their respects—members of other victims' families, and many who had been recipients of my wife's generosity. Some of them were crying so much it made us uncomfortable. Our faith teaches us to be in control near the deceased, or when visiting the dead in a cemetery. We believe that wailing does not help anyone—not the wailer, and certainly not the deceased. Allah loves our prayers, not our out-of-control wailing and mourning. It is for this reason that the excessive displays of emotion surrounding my wife were extremely distressing to us.

I saw that a diversion was necessary, to save those gathered from further pain, so I advised everyone to recite with me. Then, I asked them to join me in *du'a*, begging Allah's mercy for Husna. This prayer gave me—and everyone else—an opportunity for tears. Alongside me, my daughter cried with moderation, and I was so proud of her strength. However, I was also concerned about the pressure that controlling her emotions placed on her, so I advised her to take some time in a corner with Husna's nieces.

Afterwards, I moved along to pay my respects to the others who had died. I wanted to make *du'a* for as many of the dead as I could. As I moved from casket to casket, I waded through an ocean of tears. The whole tent was filled with the sound of crying, and if I had not had my *du'a* to turn to I might have dissolved myself.

When the announcement was made that the funeral prayer was about to commence, we assembled ourselves in straight lines. Before us stretched the line of caskets.

In my life, I have attended innumerable funerals, but never before one like this, never one where I have made *du'a* for so many. But, although the air was full of heartbreak, there was also a hopefulness about the proceedings. When I looked at the caskets, I saw heroes, people who had been true ambassadors for peace, who had died in worship. I felt proud of them, and I felt their message of peace radiating from them.

Indeed, I felt very strongly that each of those people was there with us in that tent. They were alive in our memories, and would live on throughout history. 'We are in Paradise,' I felt that they were reassuring us. 'Be peaceful like us so that you, too, may attain Paradise one day.'

The funeral prayer was deeply moving. It brought all of us together in our grief, and guided me to find the peace of mind I would need to finally bury my beloved wife. I prayed for her with my entire being, wishing for her the very best in the next life. I prayed just as fervently for the others who had died with her and who now lay before us.

I felt myself suffused with love, a love that radiated outwards without limit—the love I had for Husna grew to encompass everyone there in that tent with me, and kept growing so that I felt a deep and sincere love for all of humankind. That prayer gave me serenity. I knew that Allah would look after our loved ones as He cares for all of us. I prayed for peace, safety, security and happiness for everyone in this world.

FINALLY, IT WAS TIME TO bury my wife. All of the graves had been dug ahead of time. The volunteers called out the casket numbers one by one, then each was carried out by six people chosen by the grieving family—only six could go, due to the enormous number of people there. In my wheelchair, I was not able to carry my wife's casket, so I had to choose six people to accompany me. As our female family members stood aside to watch the burial, a surge of men swarmed me, all volunteering to carry Husna. Their lives had been touched by my wife, and they were all determined to be a part of her burial. I wish I could have let everyone who wanted to come with me do so, but I couldn't; I was forced to choose. I thanked those who remained, and reassured them that they had honoured Husna simply through their presence.

We carried Husna to her graveside. Then, at my instruction, my supporters lifted her body out of the casket and placed it carefully within the grave. In our faith, we bury only the body, not the casket. My supporters arranged my wife so that she was facing towards the qibla—this is the direction of the Kaaba (holy house) in Mecca, and is the same way that Muslims face each of the five times daily that we pray. We face the qibla no matter where in the world we are, because doing so signifies that we pray to one point: God.

Once Husna's body was arranged, we covered her with a wooden lid to keep off the earth, and then with some soil. As all this was done, we recited first the shahada (our declaration of faith), then the following verse from the Holy Quran: 'From the earth We created you, and into it We will return you, and from it We will extract you another time.' (20:55)

'*Jazaakumullah*,' I said to my supporters, grateful for their sincere assistance. *May Allah grant you rewards.*

Islam teaches us to thank those who give us help. The actual term for 'thank you' is *shukran*, but it is preferable to say *Jazakallah* (or the plural form *Jazaakumullah*) instead, as doing so offers a prayer to Allah, that He might grant the helper rewards. Prayer itself—as in, the action rather than just a word—is an even more sincere way to show thanks.

Finally, we made *du'a* for Husna. That prayer was very soothing.

My supporters left me alone beside my wife, so that I could pray and recite for her by myself, one last time.

Then I, too, turned and left.

My soul was at peace, for I knew that my beloved wife was in the best place. She was with Allah, and she would receive His mercy—a gift more precious than anything I or this world would ever be able to give her.

V

Love,
above all

22.

A true hero

As the Prophet Muhammad (peace be upon him) said,
'A true hero is the one who can control himself or herself
during anger.' (Muttafaqun A'Laih)

They give priority to others over themselves, even though
poverty is their own lot. (Al-Quran 59:9)

IT WAS ONLY AFTER MY wife was buried that I found sleep.
I was exhausted—the week between her death and her burial had
been extremely taxing on me, on Shifa and on our wider family, in
more ways than I can possibly list. When her funeral was finally
completed, all of the exhaustion that I had been pushing to the

back of my mind swamped me. The lack of sleep caught up with me. I was incapacitated. For the next week I rested and slept, and rested some more, trying to regain some small spark of energy, but what sleep I did get was of poor quality. It was the same for Shifa.

With sleep, my dreams also returned. Many were terrifying, not dreams but nightmares, in which I revisited scenes and fears that replicated what I had witnessed in person, and I was forced to re-see things I wish I had never seen in the first place. Shifa, too, had nightmares. I gave us both homeopathic remedies to treat our shock, and that helped. I also made sure we talked to one another, that we were open about our grief, so that we could process it together. That also helped, and continues to.

Not all of my dreams were frightening, however. In one, my wife came to me. The exhaustion I felt in the real world carried through to that dream, and as I lay in a hospital bed, overcome by fatigue, I saw Husna walk past the doorway to my room. I called out to her—'I'm in here! Look, here I am!'—but she did not stop. She did not even turn towards me, but I could see the side of her face, and on it she wore a cheeky grin. She kept walking, then disappeared.

When I awoke, I took the dream as a message. My wife was happy, and she was happy with me, but she was gone from this world for good. 'It is time to move on with your life,' the dream was telling me, so I did my best to listen.

THERE IS ONE THING I still do not know, will never truly know, and that is what my wife's last moments on this earth were like. I have done my best to piece together the facts of her death with what I've heard from those who saw her and with what I know of her personality, so that I have something of an idea, but my absence from her side will always cause me pain. I was not there with her, but I know she was looking for me, thinking of me, just as I was her.

When we parted ways outside Masjid al-Noor that Friday in March, we did not know that one of us was about to leave this world. We did not know that with every step Husna took away from me, she was walking closer to her death, closer to the moment our tight team of two would be split in half. In this world at least, we were about to be separated, but I wait with joy in my heart for the day that we will be reunited in Paradise.

Here is what I believe to be true: my wife paid with her life so that others would be saved. She put her own safety second to the safety of those around her. She was generous to her dying moment.

A woman who was in the prayer room with Husna later confirmed this to me. 'I was so scared, I put my head down on the ground,' she told me, 'but Husna was running in and out. She came and went three times.'

If my wife had only wanted to save herself, why would she have done this? If all she cared for was preserving her own survival, she would have run away and never gone back inside. She would have found a place of safety, and she would have hidden and prayed, and she might have lived. But that is not what Husna did. That is not the Husna I know. As always, my wife's concern for others over-rode any worries about her own safety.

When I was a child, I remember watching a hen and her many chicks on our farm. In the sky above circled a kite, which swooped down repeatedly, trying to snatch the chicks. All the while, the mother hen was running back and forth, doing everything she could to protect her babies. Her actions moved me, for in them I saw love, dedication and sacrifice. Now, when I think of Husna in the women's room on 15 March, I think of that mother hen. In that room with my wife were other women, including the elderly and infirm, and young children and babies. Husna would have done everything in her power to ensure that they were saved. I know that.

I also know that she would have been filled with worry about me. My wife, who had cared for and worried about me for over two decades, would have thought only of finding me and getting me outside. I imagine the thoughts that rushed through her head after the shooting began must have been similar to my thoughts about her. *Where is my husband? Is he OK? Has he been shot?* There was a reason that so many people had found hope in learning that I, the man in the wheelchair, had survived: they had assumed that, because I could not run away, I must have been killed. It's likely my wife feared the same thing.

I was told that she went into the main men's prayer room in her attempts to find me. She went and looked in the corner up the front where I always prayed, the place where so many people's bodies ended up piled. In that corner, someone broke a window, and through it people fled. I was also told that one young man made it out only to get hit on the head and fall unconscious. When he came to a few seconds later, he pulled himself to his feet and stood there, gazing around, confused.

'Run!' he heard a woman's voice urge him. 'What are you doing standing there? Go! It's not safe!'

He turned and looked back through the window at the owner of the voice. It was my wife.

'I took her advice, and I ran for my life,' he told me afterwards. 'She helped me to think straight. It was only once I had made it to safety that I stopped to realise that I had left Aunty Husna behind, in the place where it was unsafe. I should not have left her there. I should have pulled her out of there and made her run with me. She saved my life, but I couldn't do anything for her.'

Another man who was inside that main prayer room also said that he saw her. He had been shot in the thigh and was lying on the floor. His wound was bleeding profusely, and as the blood drained out of him so did his energy. He couldn't talk, was barely alive, when he saw my wife.

'She came in looking for you,' he told me. 'She was there just a few minutes before you came in. I tried to call out to her, but I couldn't. I couldn't do anything for her. She looked so worried. I never imagined that the shooter would kill a lady . . .'

So Husna had left the room mere moments before I appeared in it. As she headed towards the front of the mosque, I had been coming into the room from the back. In my mind's eye, I can see my brave wife in that room, searching for me despite the risk to her own life, and that vision breaks my heart and makes the tears prick at my eyes. How can it be that we missed one another? Husna's words from after my accident come back to me whenever I think of how near we came: *My sorrow is that, being so close, I could not help the person I love.* This thought leaves me feeling as helpless as I did sitting outside the mosque by my car, listening to the sounds of gunfire.

I wish that we had spotted one another, and yet it wasn't meant to be.

SO WHAT DID HUSNA DO after she had finished searching the mosque? She would not have found any sign of me. Did she hope that I had miraculously escaped? Or was she afraid she might find me wounded—or worse—somewhere else? I can only guess at what was going through her mind as she went back through the women's room, then exited out a side door and began to make her way towards Deans Avenue. I know that this is how she left because another person, lying injured inside the mosque, saw her doing just that.

She was leaving. She was going towards safety.

I like to imagine that, in those moments, her heart was filled with hope that I might have survived—after all, when I did not find *her* inside, I had been hopeful. I had hoped that meant she had escaped. I hope she knew I was alive.

It was as she departed that my wife was shot in the back.

In her final moments, I hope you are able to see everything I have already told you of my wife: her bravery, her strength, and her incredible capacity to hope and to love even when faced with the worst this world can offer.

AS IT TURNED OUT, I came close to my wife one more time that Friday at the mosque, but even if I had seen her by then it would have been too late. When the police officers found me inside the prayer room and escorted me out, they took me through the side gate. If I had gone out through the middle gate, I would have seen my wife lying dead where she had fallen.

I do not know how I would have handled it if I had seen her there.

I do not know why Allah decided to keep me from seeing her there.

I do not know why He wanted me to have to wait, anxiously, and search for a little longer before I learned what had become of her.

But I do know that, whatever His reasons, His decision was for the best.

IT IS NOT OFTEN THAT the world offers us heroes. They are a rare and precious breed relegated all too commonly to the stories we tell our children. We forget that they exist among us, that often our most noble heroes are hiding in plain sight. A true hero is not showy, does not need to tell you they are heroic, because their actions speak for them. You might, therefore, not even recognise a hero when you see one. They tend to be the people you least expect.

Seeing a hero—a true, selfless, loving hero—is an act of positivity. It is an act of power. In order to see the good, you have to look for it. It's also an act that will ask you to be brave, to be determined, because too often the world we live in would prefer that you dwell on the bad.

My wife, Husna Ahmed, was a hero.

She risked her life to save others.

She died trying to save me.

To her final breath, she was hopeful, hard-working, brave and loving.

In our Muslim community, it's generally accepted that men should take care of women. When we make our marriage vows, a husband commits to providing for his wife. Our faith is not unique in this regard—many cultures and beliefs hold similar notions. Many of us the world over believe that men will risk, and even give, their lives to save women and children. When a ship is sinking, the first rescue boats are dedicated to the women and the young. We rarely consider that things might go the other way, and yet that's precisely the position my brave wife found herself in on her final day on this earth. She acted with unparalleled bravery, putting her life at risk in order to save others. In order to save me.

Husna's triumph over me, her loving husband, was total that day. It had begun with her quick fingers swiftly fixing the mess I had made of the tassel on my trousers—*It's just a little knot*, I can still hear her saying. *An easy thing to fix*—and it was confirmed in those final moments before she died. She came to rescue me. She gave her precious life for me. How can I ever compete with that?

The bravery, love and optimism that drove her was that of a mother protecting her children. Husna, the mother of our beloved daughter, was a mother to all, a hero, the very best of us.

23.
Forgiveness

O you who believe! Al-Qisas [the law of equality in punishment] is prescribed for you in case of murder: the free for the free, the slave for the slave, and the female for the female. But if the killer is forgiven by the brother [or the relatives] of the killed against blood-money, then adhering to it with fairness and payment of the blood-money to the heir should be made in fairness. This is an alleviation and a mercy from your Lord. So after this whoever transgresses the limits [kills the killer after taking the blood-money], he shall have a painful torment. (Al-Quran 2:178)

The recompense for an injury [or evil] is an injury [or evil]
equal to it [in degree], but if a person forgives and makes
reconciliation, his reward is due from Allah. (Al-Quran 42:40)

And hasten to forgiveness from your Lord and a garden as
wide as the heavens and earth, prepared for the righteous
who spend [in the cause of Allah] during ease and hardship
and who restrain anger and who pardon the people: Verily,
Allah loves those who do good. (Al-Quran 3:133–4)[1]

IN THE AFTERMATH OF THE attack, I spoke to many, many
people who had been there in Masjid al-Noor with me that day. They
all had stories to share, were all devastated, and among them were the
people who helped me stitch together my wife's final movements.

Also among them were the people I had seen outside on Deans
Avenue while I searched in vain for my wife, still believing she was
alive somewhere. I asked many people that day if they had seen
Husna, if they knew where she was, and all of them told me the
same thing: even if they had seen her at some point, they did not
know what had happened to her. But that was not, in all cases, true.
Some of them *had* already seen my wife's body, face down on the
concrete, but they could not find the words to tell me the news,
not then. I never realised that, while I was choosing not to tell the

---

1   Here, verse 2:178 shows us that forgiveness is an option Allah has prescribed in
    the Holy Quran. (The translation of this verse is taken from *Interpretation of the
    Meanings of the Noble Quran in the English Language* by Dr Muhammad Taqi-ud-
    Din Al-Hilali and Dr Muhammad Muhsin Khan.) Verse 42:40 shows us that
    forgiveness is a better option, given preference in the Holy Quran, and verses
    3:133–4 show us that Allah loves forgiveness.

people whose loved ones I had seen dead in case I made a horrible mistake, others were doing the exact same thing to me.

Indeed, while I was busy searching for Husna out there on Deans Avenue, news of her death had already made it to social media. One of the photos posted with the early news reports showed what appeared to be my wife's lifeless body lying on the footpath by our mosque. Many people saw it before I even knew she was dead, and they knew it was her. Of course, I had no phone, so there was no way I would have seen it. Later in the evening on 15 March, someone showed me that picture. The image is seared into my brain.

In the weeks after the attack, more than one person wanted to apologise to me.

'I am so sorry I did not tell you,' they each said. 'I knew your wife had been killed. I had seen her. But I could not tell you. I was too scared to break your heart.'

When my Muslim brothers and sisters begged my forgiveness, I willingly forgave them. I did not blame them.

'You did what you thought was best for both me and for yourself,' I said to them. 'Thank you.'

I understood perfectly why they had done what they did. I had, after all, done the same thing myself. And what would blaming have got me, anyway? It certainly would not have brought my Husna back to me. It was easy to forgive. It cost me nothing, and it saved me from further grief. It was the best thing to do.

THERE IS ONE MORE PERSON I have forgiven after the terrible events of that day: the man who killed my wife.

One day after the attack on our mosque, a reporter asked me,

'What is your feeling towards the killer of your wife?'

The question caught me off guard, and I answered spontaneously. 'I love him as a human brother, but I do not support what he did.'

I explained that I had forgiven him, that it was what Husna would have wanted.

Then, a couple of weeks later on 29 March, a remembrance service was held in Hagley Park, and I was asked to speak. There, I reiterated my message of love and forgiveness.

'I don't want to have a heart that is boiling like a volcano,' I said. 'A volcano has anger, fury, rage. It doesn't have peace. It has hatred, it burns itself within, and it burns its surroundings. I don't want to have a heart like this, and I believe no one does. I want a heart that is full of love and care, and full of mercy, and will forgive lavishly, because this heart doesn't want any more life to be lost. This heart doesn't like that any human being should go through the pain I have gone through. That's why I have chosen peace, love, and I have forgiven.'

Thanks to the media and the internet, that speech found an audience far further afield than just my home city of Christchurch, and I soon received another invitation—this time, to attend an assembly in Washington, D.C. So, a few months later on 16 July, I found myself at the 2019 Ministerial to Advance Religious Freedom, as one of three speakers in the first segment of the first day. To the assembled delegates, I reiterated my message that we are all part of one human family, and that we must embrace one another as brothers and sisters, showing love and respect, not hate and violence. Later, at the White House, I shook the hand of the President of the United States as a gesture of peace and harmony.

I was one of a group of 27 survivors of religious persecution invited to attend the ministerial, and afterwards I had many delegates approach me to praise New Zealand's compassionate response to the 15 March attack.

Then, in mid-November, I travelled to the Netherlands to attend the seventh meeting of the Istanbul Process in the Hague and participate in a panel discussion titled 'Incitement to Religious Hatred and Violence: Push Back'. In his opening speech, the Minister of Foreign Affairs of the Kingdom of the Netherlands, Stef Blok, welcomed me personally. 'Mr Ahmed,' he said, 'thank you so much for travelling so far to be with us today. I believe your presence here is very important, because you showed us that there is hope. That love can triumph over hate. And today, we face a number of challenging questions: How can we preserve and spread that message? How can we ensure that people around the world are not subject to violence, discrimination or intimidation, because of their faith? Or, indeed, because of their lack of faith? What can we learn from each other?'

I have continued to receive invitations to speak. In early December 2019 I travelled to the United Arab Emirates to attend the Sixth Assembly of the Forum for Promoting Peace, and to contribute on the topic 'The Role of Religions in Promoting Tolerance: From Possibility to Necessity'.

I say yes to every invite I am able to. I see each one as a gift from Allah, an opportunity to spread my message of love and forgiveness as far and wide as possible. I have learned, in the aftermath of the attack in which my wife was killed, just how desperately our world thirsts for this message. Too often the messages we receive are of hate and fear, and all we need is to be shown another way. That's why I will do everything within my ability to spread peace.

ONE SUNDAY LATER IN 2019, a new couple arrived in one of the Quran classes I have continued to take at Masjid al-Noor since Husna's death. It was their first time attending, and before everyone had left at the end of the class, the man stood up and addressed me.

'My wife and I are from Iraq,' he said, 'and I have a question for you, Brother Farid. It's a question I'd like to ask you in front of the class, because I'd like everyone to hear the answer.'

'Of course,' I replied. 'Please, what is your question?'

'Why did you do it?'

I was a little confused. 'I'm sorry. What do you mean? Are you referring to the idea to do no harm?' I thought he was talking about the topic of that day's class, and I was already mentally preparing a reply when he interrupted my thoughts.

'No, no. Not that. I mean, why did you forgive your wife's killer?'

I did not have to think before I replied. 'Why not?'

The man just watched me, so I went on. 'You are from Iraq,' I said. 'You tell me what reasons you would have *not* to forgive those who have hurt you.'

He gave this some reflection, then said, 'The Holy Quran tells us that if one man kills another it is as though he has killed all of mankind. On 15 March, a gunman took fifty-one lives. It is as though he has killed all of us, fifty-one times over. So why did you forgive him?'

Now I understood where he was coming from. He was referring to the passage that tells us 'whoever kills a soul, unless for a soul or for corruption [done] in the land, it is as if he had slain mankind entirely. And whoever saves one, it is as if he had saved mankind entirely.' (5:32) I smiled.

'That particular quote creates two categories,' I said. 'In one is the killer. In the other is the victim. The killer has commited a terrible wrong, and he is responsible for his wrongdoing. But my question should be, "What are the rights given to me by God to respond to the killing of my wife?" Well, Islam gives me three options. One is to demand equal punishment, or Qisas. Second, I can demand compensation. Or, finally, I can forgive the killer of my wife without making any demands. My brother, I have chosen the third option: forgiveness.' Then I cited a few verses from the Holy Quran to support my position.

The man was silent, pondering this. Then he spoke again. 'Your logic is interesting,' he said. 'I had not thought about it like that. But let's check what my wife thinks . . .'

His wife, who had been quietly listening along with everyone else in the class, smiled at me.

'She was a professor at an Islamic university back in Iraq. She's extremely well versed in the Holy Quran and its interpretations.'

'Oh!' I replied. 'Well, why didn't you say so sooner?'

But I was still smiling at him, and he was smiling, too. Of course I knew why he had kept his wife's credentials secret: he had wanted to see what I would say first.

Now, let me tell you what his wife said to me. 'Your level of faith, Mr Ahmed, is not down here—' she tapped the top of a desk with the flat of her hand, then lifted it high above her head—'it is up here.'

Her words brought tears to my eyes. It was not the praise of myself that moved me; it was having a person of such wisdom praise my faith and my interpretation of my religion. Nothing I do is for myself. I do not want to spread a message of love in order to make myself look good. I do it to help others, to guide us all towards a more peaceful and loving world.

THAT IRAQI MAN IS JUST one of many, many, many people who have asked me, 'Why do you forgive your wife's killer?' Perhaps you are asking that question yourself. There are inevitably other questions, too—was it difficult, at what stage did I decide to forgive, did I have to give it much consideration, and so on. I don't mind these questions. They are the product of human curiosity, which is the root of learning. These questions show that people want to understand how to forgive. It's a question I take very seriously, and one I want to answer with care.

The truth is that I forgave him because it was the obvious thing to do. It was a natural response to me. I forgave immediately, but that action was the product of many years' living and learning.

My whole life I have done my best to channel all of my efforts in one direction: love. For 24 years, I was married to a woman whose direction was exactly the same. For both me and Husna it has always been natural to respond with love, and where necessary to show that love through forgiveness. So, just as my wife unconditionally forgave the man who ran me over with his car and put me in a wheelchair, I know she would have wished for me to forgive her killer.

My faith tells me that humans all come from the same place—we have one creator, and we are descended from one human pair. In the Holy Quran, Allah says, 'O mankind, indeed We have created you from male and female and made you peoples and tribes that you may know one another. Indeed, the most noble of you in the sight of Allah is the most righteous of you.' (49:13) We are many and various, but we are related to one another by our humanity. We form one big family—the family of humankind. For all our diversity, we are still human brothers and sisters. We all have feelings in our hearts, we are all born, and we all die. We share the same earth as our home. We breathe the same air and bask under the same sun.

This is what I have taught my many students over the years, and it is why I encourage others to treat their human brothers and sisters with love, respect and fairness above all else. When, on 15 March 2019, the killer brought his gun and his hate into our mosque, he murdered his brothers and sisters. What he did was inhumane, but even so he is still a human. He is therefore, in my eyes, still my brother—albeit one who did a terrible thing to our shared family. It is this sense of God-given brotherhood that compels me to forgive him. That is the course of action I choose.

On that day, that man made his own choice: to make a murderer of himself. He took the lives of 51 innocent people, and wounded so many more. In doing so, he inflicted the most grievous wound of all on his own soul. One day, he too will die, as we all must. And where do we go when that happens? I know where I am going, thanks to my faith. I believe that, on the Day of Judgement, my good actions and my bad actions will be laid out before me, as the Holy Quran tells me: 'That Day, the people will depart separated [into categories] to be shown [the result of] their deeds. So whoever does an atom's weight of good will see it, And whoever does an atom's weight of evil will see it.' (99:6–8) All human souls will face this judgement. It is upon the merits of our actions, and thanks to Allah's mercy, that we might gain entry to Paradise. I know that is where Husna is waiting for me, and my desire to once again be by her side guides me to be good in every way I humanly can.

The killer, however, was so driven by hate and fear that he failed to see how his actions might follow him beyond this life and into the next. How heavily will his evils weigh upon his soul? Allah alone knows that. As it is said in the Holy Quran, if a person kills one innocent person, it is as though they are killing all of humankind. The killer's act was an attack on humanity, of which he forgot that he himself is part. In harming others, he also harmed himself. He failed to understand the true consequences of his wrongdoing. Perhaps he believed that, by killing our loved ones, he was punishing them or somehow disadvantaging them. If so, I wish he realised how truly mistaken he was. Yes, he took 51 innocent lives. Yes, he left many others bleeding and wounded. His crimes harmed bodies and broke hearts, but they had no impact on the salvation of his victims' souls.

As Muslims, we believe that Friday is the best day, that Jumu'ah is the best prayer, and that a mosque is the best place—so, all 51 people that day died in the best place, on the best of days. They lost their lives, but they did not lose the reward of Paradise. Our martyred husbands and wives and mothers and fathers and sons and daughters and aunties and uncles are safe in the mercy of Allah.

NO ONE OWNS A MOSQUE. It is a house of Allah, and its doors are open to all—a grace that the killer took awful advantage of on 15 March. When he entered Masjid al-Noor, he was apparently greeted with respect and love.

'Hello, brother,' it seems that the man at the door said.

That man was the first victim of the shootings.

The killer did not value the sanctity of human life. He listened to hate, and hate told him to kill. Hate did not tell him the stories of the lives he took. He did not consider that he was killing people who mattered, people with skills they contributed to their communities, people who ran businesses and had PhDs and loved their families. He killed hard-working, peace-loving, caring Kiwis. He did not respect their lives, and he did not respect their home. He did not know their names. He did not think their lives were precious.

But the lives of others *are* precious. I know that. I am not a killer. I am not driven by hate. When I went back into our mosque and saw the destruction that man had wrought, I vowed to do whatever I could to counteract his actions of hate with a message of love and forgiveness. I did not want any more lives to be lost. I prayed the violence would stop there.

I knew that many would be angry about what he had done, and I could understand why. Anyone with a heart would feel extremely upset by such atrocity. An attack such as that visited on our mosque and the one in Linwood seeks to inspire anger. It is an act born of hate, and it wants to spread hate. It wants to make people fearful, angry, hurt—but if we let those feelings guide us, things can only get worse. I wanted to do what I could to bring that hate to a halt.

I HAVE ALWAYS BEEN KIND-HEARTED—sometimes to my detriment, in the eyes of others. But I do not see kindness as the weakness that others might. I believe it to be a strength.

Some of us are born with kind hearts, while others may have to find a way towards kindness. I see kindness as a jewel, and I wear mine gratefully. When making jewellery, a goldsmith removes impurities; likewise, if we wish to be truly kind, we must cleanse our hearts of impurities. For kindness is the total absence of hate, cruelty, anger, pettiness, intolerance, jealousy and selfishness. So long as our hearts hide these impurities, it will be impossible for us to be truly kind.

My parents have many stories of my kindness as a child, and so do my relatives and family friends, but often their stories are framed by worry that I might be too sensitive, or that my kindness might be taken advantage of. And their concerns have not always been ill-placed, as being kind has frequently asked sacrifice of me. I remember once, when I was a child, a boy who was my neighbour came crying to me, saying he did not have any money. Well, my sensitive heart could not bear that, so I found a way to help him— and then later discovered that he had used my money to buy cigarettes. But I did not mind. What mattered was that I had acted out of kindness, not what someone then went and did with that generosity. I have never begrudged the sacrifices I have made in the service of kindness. I believe that Allah is kind, and He loves me to be kind too. I also believe that, if I am kind to His creations, then He will be kind to me. As the Holy Prophet Muhammad (peace be upon him) said, 'Be kind to the inhabitants on earth, then [the God] in heaven will be kind to you.' (Abu Dawood and Tismidi)

What the killer did on 15 March 2019 was unkind, cruel, the most lowly of actions, but that could not change who I am. I was kind before that man killed my wife and 50 other innocents, and I am still kind. I want to continue to be kind. The killer's unkindness cannot make me unkind, and that is why I offer him my kindness in the form of forgiveness.

Being kind has always precluded me from the capacity to hate, to see another human as my enemy. I do not hate anyone, and never have, not even when people have done things that have hurt me. When I was a child, I felt things very deeply—if I and my friends had an altercation of any sort, I would feel saddened and cry. However, that was all I did. Even if someone was unkind to me, I still wished them well. My focus has always centred on being compassionate and loving, so there is simply no room for hate.

And hate did not suddenly take hold of me the day that my wife was killed by a hate-filled man. I felt sad, devastated, heartbroken, but I did not feel hate. How could I? I had never felt it before, and did not wish to start. The killer might have hated those of us who had come together in peaceful worship, but that did not mean I should hate him back. I did not want revenge. I forgave him so that hate would not take up residence in my already hurting heart.

AS A NATURAL EXTENSION OF my incapacity to hate, I do not believe any of my human brothers or sisters to be my enemy. Enmity is as foreign to my heart as hate is. To me, it is a waste of energy. All I can ask is, 'Why?'

Who says I have to be anyone's enemy?

What benefit will that possibly bring me, or anyone else?

The answers are self-evident: no one, and none.

Throughout my life, there have been people who have not agreed with me or who have actively disliked me—of course there have. Sometimes I have found myself on the receiving end of unfair or hurtful criticism, or facing aggressive opposition. It is all OK with me. The way I see it, another person's dislike opens the door to good: if we step through it, we can use it as an opportunity for discussion, for learning from one another. And, if the worst comes to pass and someone else takes me as their enemy, I do not reciprocate. Instead, I pray for peace, harmony, understanding, and I continue to be a caring friend. I do not want to be any person's enemy.

I know that Husna felt the same. She was a friend to one and all. She was unfailingly kind. Up until the moment that she died, she treated others with love. She did not hold hate in any part of her being.

We are all different, in so many ways, and that means it's natural to have different opinions about things. Our differences are cause for celebration, not for discord and enmity. Just because someone believes something different from you, or doesn't want to do things how you would do them, that does not mean you have to dislike one another. Our differences need not make enemies of us. Rather, we should see them as the precious assets they are.

Our differences are what give colour and vibrancy to our vast, rich, wonderful world; without them, this life would be dull and grey. Every single one of us is unique, and has something special to contribute to our big human family. When we are kind to one another, when we are open to befriending those who might otherwise be enemies, we give that uniqueness room to grow and flourish and make us all stronger. On the other hand, if we give in to anger and fear by seeing others as enemies, we will only hurt each other.

When the killer attacked our mosques, he was acting on the misplaced idea that the worshippers within were his enemies. This despite the fact that we never had any enmity or dispute with him. How could I? How could any of those peaceful worshippers? We had no idea who he was.

Allah alone knows the true cause of that man's hate, of his sense of enmity, but it evidently sprang from a fear of difference. In spite of the death and awful harm he caused out of hate, I still do not think of him as my enemy. If he saw me as his enemy, I answer that feeling with forgiveness. I am not his enemy.

MOST SIGNIFICANTLY, MY FORGIVENESS is inspired by the divine forgiveness of the Prophet Muhammad (peace be upon him), who prayed to Allah to forgive wrongdoers their mistakes. It is reported that, upon telling the story of a prophet who was beaten by his people, the Prophet said, 'My Lord, forgive my people for they do not know.' (Muttafaqun A'Laih)

This is a powerful truth.

There are many prophets (peace be upon them all) who have taken the approach of forgiving wrongdoers on the basis that they know not what they do. Honourable messengers of God such as Jacob, Joseph, Moses, Jesus and others won people's hearts through compassion, and guided us towards righteousness and goodness. They forgave people lavishly. Allah advised His last Prophet,

Muhammad (peace be upon him), and his followers: 'Show forgiveness [on your part], instruct what is right, but turn away from those who are ignorant.' (Al-Quran 7:199)

The prophets came to educate us, to teach us how to love one another, not to hate or destroy one another. Through their own actions, they provided an example of how to forgive. They dedicated their lives to helping wrongdoers transform into proponents of good. They showed us that forgiveness is the force that halts the destruction vendetta sows. They showed us that forgiveness is not weakness but rather the most powerful action for winning hearts. They taught us that forgiveness is the most beneficial action for peace among humankind. Forgiveness is the path to peace.

This truth—that wrongdoers do not fully comprehend the gravity of their actions—is something I think about often. It is a message that I admire, and that I seek to embody in the way I live my own life. I try to remind myself that people who do wrong simply do not realise they are being guided by wrongful knowledge; consequently, they believe that what they are doing is right. When I remember this, I am able to feel sad for wrongdoers instead of angry at them. I feel sorry for them. My wife shared this sympathy. 'The poor guy,' she said of the young man who ran me over, while I was still in the hospital. 'He must have had a bad day.'

Our wise daughter has also shown sympathy to wrongdoers. At the age of fifteen, she said of the man who killed her dear mother, 'Poor man. Perhaps he was hurt badly, and has chosen hate instead of love.'

The attack of 15 March 2019 tested my compassion like nothing in my life beforehand, not even the terrible accident that left me wheelchair-bound. By showing sympathy, I do not mean to make excuses for the killer or his horrible actions. I show sympathy because I do not want to let his bad actions make me bad. The killer committed a terrible action, one that did no favour to anyone. He hurt everyone, including himself. He killed so many people, and he left those who survived with untold physical and emotional scars. Furthermore, he wounded the souls of every compassionate Kiwi who saw what he had done and understood that there was no undoing it.

He knew that his actions would lead to death and despair, and yet he went ahead with them. He was guided by the false idea that his actions were 'right', were somehow in line with the wrongful knowledge that had filled his head. I have heard that the killer aligned himself with extreme right-wing ideas, including describing himself as an 'ethnonationalist'—a form of nationalism that aligns nation-hood with race. Presumably he believed his whiteness made him superior to others, but this sort of racist thinking is a no-win. A person who believes that their race (however they choose to define it) makes them better than others is engaged in a war that can never end. No one will ever win that battle, and everyone will suffer.

Racism is a product of hate, so it has no home in my soul. I have always been surrounded by people from all sorts of backgrounds and all tiers of society, and this diversity has taught me to offer every person the same level of respect. We all come from different places, and have different cultures—that is a fact of the world we live in. We can love the things that make us and our cultures different from others, but that love does not lead to hate. True love can never logically lead to hate. That is why racist ideas, which say our differences make 'us' better and 'them' worse, will never lead to peace or to happiness. They will only create hurt, anger, disunity.

Five times a day, I pray to Allah for peace and love for all, and doing so reminds me of my kinship with every other person on this earth. When I pray at mosque, I line up alongside worshippers who come from all over the world, who speak many different languages, who represent many cultures, who occupy all kinds of places in society. Side by side, humbled, we pray together. In the eyes of God, every one of us is the same—rich and poor, king and cleaner, leader and layperson, we all pray in the same way. Our prayer reminds us of our shared existence, of our shared pursuit of goodness. Praying in unity buries the notion of racism. How could the idea that one race is better than another possibly find a foothold in such an act of love and solidarity?

In worship, we come together to pray for the best, and for the wisdom to conduct ourselves righteously. And what is righteousness? It is love, kindness, generosity, respect, sincerity, honesty, fairness. It is a recognition of our shared and fundamental human rights. It is the opposite of racism.

If the killer had properly understood the true nature of things, he would have known that no human should kill their fellow human. If he had properly understood, he would have realised his sense of enmity was one-sided. If he had properly understood, he would have seen that differences are something to be embraced, not erased. Perhaps if he had known these truths he would have thought twice before making himself a murderer. Perhaps he would have lowered his gun. Perhaps he would have walked into our mosque and met the warm greeting he received with a 'Hello, brother' of his own.

But that is not what he did.

Somehow, he misunderstood everything that is good, loving and kind, even when it was standing at the door to welcome him into a place of peace. He was so utterly misguided by hate and anger that he disappeared off down a dark and hateful path that hurt one and all.

WHEN I CONSIDER ALL OF this, I can only feel sympathy for that man. I truly wish for him to find the correct knowledge, to see the truth, to discover the learning that will show him how to set his life upon the correct path. I pray for him, pray that he will find divine guidance so as to save himself and others from further suffering. I do this because it's what my compassionate wife would have done. I do it because I follow the Prophet Muhammad (peace be upon him), who was sent by Allah as a mercy for mankind.

I do not wish to be a hateful, angry man with murder and blood on my mind. I want to follow in the forgiving and loving footsteps of those who are the very best of us.

If there is any good to come of such a devastating tragedy as that which occurred in Christchurch on 15 March 2019, I hope it is this: I hope that it provokes all of us who live on this planet together and look up at the same night sky to set our personal compasses in the direction of love. I hope it shows us why we must turn away from hate, why we must orientate ourselves towards what is best.

My hopes are not unfounded: the response of Kiwis everywhere, of people from all walks of life, to this tragedy showed that hate does not have to triumph. The people of New Zealand shared our personal grief as their own, and they extended their heartfelt love with a compassion so immense that it burst outwards from our remote country and touched people and nations all over the world.

I believe that our response—our ability to halt hate with love—will inspire many others to open their hearts and their minds. I believe it will guide people to seek wisdom in their relationships with their human brothers and sisters. I believe it will inspire them to stop killing, to stop hating, and to instead start loving one another.

I have good reason to believe this, because I can already see it happening all around me.

24.

Choose love

And not equal are the good deed and the bad. Repel [evil]
by that [deed] which is better. (Al-Quran 41:34)

As the Prophet Muhammad (peace be upon him) said,
'Allah does not bestow His mercy on a person who does not
show mercy to other humans.' (Muttafaqun A'Laih)

LET ME ASK YOU THIS: if one person commits a cruelty, will
another cruelty fix the problem?

No, it won't. Not really.

Just because someone does something unutterably wrong,
that does not justify answering that wrong with more wrong.

Combatting hate with hate will only breed more hate. If we do that, where does the hate stop?

There is one way to break a cycle of hate, and that is to reverse it. Meet hate with love, and goodness will overcome anything the wrong seeks to achieve. Love is the water we pour on the fire of hate; when the two meet, the lesser fizzles and dies. So, when someone commits an act of hate, respond with love. Put out that fire. As the Holy Quran tells us, we should face evil with what is best. That means allowing wrongdoers the chance to be corrected, to be educated. It means putting love to work in order to learn from others' wrongdoing, so that we might ensure such things are not repeated. This is how hate is expelled by love. It is how we might find hope in even the most hopeless of circumstances.

When we love unconditionally, we will also see the path to forgiveness. We will understand that forgiveness is the method by which we cleanse our own souls of any hate that might linger because of the cruelty done to us. When we say 'I forgive', we unburden ourselves of the compulsion to keep on hating. We break the cycle of hate. As the English poet Alexander Pope famously said many centuries ago, 'To err is human, to forgive divine.' Forgiveness is, as an extension of love, an act of divinity.

Many people conflate forgiving someone's actions with condoning them. They are not the same thing. When you forgive someone, you are not saying you think that what they did was OK. You are simply forgiving them. Their mistakes remain mistakes, their wrongdoing is still wrong. I might forgive the man who killed my wife, but I can never condone his actions. Forgiveness does not give him the licence to kill more, and nor is it sending a message that Muslims' lives are not precious. Rather, forgiveness is a power that derives from true love: its aim is to inspire others to also practise forgiveness, in order to rid the world of hate and violence and give peace to everyone.

Husna and the 50 others who died by a gunman's hand might have been in the best place on the best day, but they were killed—and killing is the worst of acts. They came together in peace and love to worship at our two mosques. Their motivations were the opposite of the man who killed them. He committed a horrendous crime. He oppressed his victims by taking their right to life, by killing them while they exercised their right to peace. Killing them was not a thing he ever had a right to do.

Where hate destroys peace, love restores it. To hate is to suffer. It is in our own best interests to avoid that suffering, to instead choose to love. We choose love so that we might know peace, and so that the world might know it by extension.

Peace is not just a job for our leaders. It is a job for each and every one of us.

OUR CREATOR GIFTED US WITH freedom of choice. This gift is a mark of respect, but it is also a responsibility. It is up to us, and us alone, to exercise our choice wisely. Will it be love or hate? Kindness or cruelty? Generosity or stinginess? Forgiveness or vengeance?

Just as we alone choose, we alone shall also bear the consequences of our choices, be they wise or misguided. Unwise decisions will inevitably lead to suffering, for which our creator is not responsible. The person who makes poor decisions has chosen their path, and they therefore choose the suffering. In doing so, they abuse their creator's generous gift of free choice.

For my part, I am grateful for the choice that my creator has given me, and I do my best to wield that freedom wisely and responsibly. That is why I choose love, not hate. What good reason could there possibly be for choosing hate over love? Hate begets hate. Hate is not good for the health. Hate borrows troubles. Hate does not reap recognition or honour. The man who killed my wife chose hate, and what good did he achieve? As far as I can tell, his actions were of no benefit to him or to anyone else. He did not receive any honour or reward for what he did. He just caused suffering.

Hate is a poor choice. I will not choose it for myself, and I do not recommend any other human choose it either. According to my faith, hate is a sin, forbidden by Allah. And, unless we repent or change our ways, we will be punished for our sins in the next life. By contrast, love is a good deed—a truth confirmed by my faith, and also universally accepted. In Islam, love is the best of deeds, a divine act. We love because God is loving, and He loves those who love His creations as He does. He will reward those who practise love in this life and in the next.

True love is divine. It is an act of charity according to the teachings of Islam. In fact, every good deed is considered a charity in our faith and, as such, is rewarded by Allah. Charity is something that we extend to others unquestioningly and without expectation. It does not cost us anything, and it can only reap benefits. Every human heart holds the capacity for love. The option to love exists within each of us; it simply rests with us to choose it. Love is, above all, the best of choices.

Love can take many forms, and there were so many examples of this in the wake of that man's hate-fuelled killing spree. The police and the paramedics who raced straight to the crime scenes chose love. The two officers who pulled over the killer's car and arrested him just 21 minutes after the first emergency call, putting themselves at great personal risk, chose love. The doctors, nurses and other medical staff who worked tirelessly to care for the influx of dead, dying and wounded in the aftermath of the attack chose love. The neighbours who opened their doors to survivors chose love. The politicians who acknowledged our loss and grieved with us chose love. The volunteers who organised so quickly to help in whatever way they could chose love. Every single Kiwi who felt our wounds as their own, whose hearts broke with ours, chose love.

The Muslim community also chose love. We greeted the killer's hate with the same grace that was shown by our brother at the door of Masjid al-Noor. Our leaders responded to hate with love, patience and tolerance. We said 'Salaam', and opened our hearts for peace.

Every single person who chooses love is a hero. Love is a brave choice, and one that so many of us have made. Our choice has been admired all over the world, because it has shown others that love, not hate, is the key to peace, safety, security and prosperity for all.

WHEN I FORGAVE THE MAN who killed my wife, I was choosing love. Hate is like a wall: if you kick it, it kicks you right back. Love, by contrast, is like a warm smile that passes between two people in a crowded room—before long that one shared smile has multiplied, jumping from two people to four, then to more, until the whole room is grinning. Love fills others with joy. Love gives security to little children. Love between human brothers and sisters has the power to bring an end to revenge, violence, killing.

Love spreads outwards like a halo, embracing everyone who falls within its glow and igniting their hearts. When we choose love, we choose to spread all the good that comes with it—and that good is never more sorely needed than in the wake of tragedy. Hate flounders in a place where love has spread, but true love survives in even the worst of scenarios, for it is housed within our hearts and minds. Even in our deepest grief, we retain the capacity to love, because we always hold the choice our creator gave us in our two hands. I know this because of the love I have seen since 15 March.

When I chose love and forgiveness, I was also making a plea: Let us spread love, not hate. The opposite of forgiveness would be vengeance, but what would revenge bring me? What would it bring any of us? It will not bring peace. It cannot bring us anything but suffering that goes on and on and on for as long as our quest for recompense continues. Forgiveness is the best tool available to us to break the chain of hate.

My message of love and forgiveness is all-encompassing. It extends to every person on this earth, including the man who murdered my wife. I do not believe that anyone should hate him, though they might detest his actions. He chose hate, but that does not mean we should make the same choice. Hate is a murderer's choice. Do we really want to make the same choices that a killer makes? I do not. I pray for the killer, that he might one day repent and be saved. In the meantime, I also forgive him, because I do not wish to hold on to any of the hate that his actions and their consequences want to burden me with. I prefer to love, and to hope that one day he might be saved. I do not want to destroy life as he did, but to preserve it.

If every one of us chose love over hate, we would change our world together. Can you imagine? In a world full of love, there would be no violence, no fear. No one would be forced to suffer the pain that I have felt at the loss of my wife, a pain I would not wish on any person. I lost my beautiful wife because of hate. My life will never be the same again, and every day I am reminded of Husna's absence. Without her, I feel empty. Husna was my true love, the mother of my daughter, my best and closest friend. Nothing will heal the scar that her death scored; it will always be red, uncomfortable and painful. However, even the worst action of hate could never erase our love. I am still in love with my wife. I feel her with me in spirit—she is with me when I pray, when I dream, as I write this.

Our love lives on after death.

Perhaps creating an entirely loving and generous world, a place where hate no longer holds any sway, is ambitious, but I hope for it nonetheless. I see that hope in others who choose love, like I do. I know there are many of you out there who want the same.

WHEN I WAS YOUNG, I used to lie down on my verandah and look up at the night sky. As I basked in the pale glow of the moon, I marvelled at the generosity of the natural world.

Is the moon's light limited to just one group of people?

Is only one country allowed to enjoy the sun's heat?

Does oxygen enter the lungs of only those who are healthy, and no one else?

Does the ocean let only one kind of boat sail upon its waves?

Nature does not know limits in the way that humans enforce them. It offers its resources freely and unconditionally.

Our heart, if we let it be, is much the same. Any limits that lie within it are of our own making. In its most pure form, love is as limitless as the cool moonlight. But, since humans often want to try to contain powers that are greater than them, many of us place limits on our love. When we do this, love stops being love, and becomes something else.

'I will only love you if you love me in return,' we might say, 'and, if you don't, I will withhold my love.'

That is not love. That is possessiveness.

Or perhaps we might mutter, 'Why should I love him? He does not agree with me. He is not part of my group.'

That is not love. That is unkindness.

In both examples, it is fear talking, not love. We are using feeble excuses—of family, or race, or politics, or nationality, or religion, or class, or whatever difference it is that we don't want to embrace—to limit our love, and in so doing we are forcing it to warp and bend. In the space where love was, something else will appear. Hate-driven traits such as envy, selfishness, rage and unkindness are like weeds in a garden. If left unchecked, they run rampant, suffocating love and goodness. They take up the space where other, more nurturing plants might have grown, and everyone suffers.

Like any family, our big shared human family is comprised of all sorts of people. There are those who live for good, and those who let themselves be waylaid by evil. That does not mean the good should strike out the bad. No. Rather we should try to win over the hearts of the misguided by showing love and kindness, and by offering help and the chance to learn and repent.

I take my duty as a member of our human family very seriously, and that is why I will not limit my love for anyone, no matter what. All humans need love, and should share it with one another. My love for the good people in my life is a form of gratitude, whereas my love for those who have harmed me is a form of hope. I want those who have done bad to have the opportunity to see the error of their ways, and to correct themselves. I believe we all have a right to learn from our mistakes.

To limit love is to commit a folly that ignores love's true nature. There are no bounds to love, and we can use it in various ways for various people. For instance, we love our parents and we love our spouses, but we do so in different ways. Likewise, we love our children and friends and relatives and colleagues, all in different ways. We can love one person and then another and another, and at no point is the love depleted. It only grows. It can be nurtured, and indeed it must. There is no need to limit love.

WHEN SOMEONE HATES YOU, IT is easy to hate them back. If someone doesn't respect your rights, or abuses you, or wants to fight you, you might want to respond in kind. Responding negatively to a negative action doesn't take any hard work. It doesn't ask any thought or reflection; it just demands a reaction that mimics the harm.

By contrast, responding *positively* to a negative action takes effort. It is not easy. Showing patience, tolerance, respect and kindness to those who have hurt you requires dedicated practice. We are told in the Holy Quran to repel evil with what is best, but that does not mean it is easy guidance to follow. It is a practice that requires, above all, self-control.

In order to maintain some sense of order, every civil society and every organised religion asks some level of self-control from its members. Self-control is what gives us the ability to stop and choose the best course of action in any given situation. In the pause enforced by our self-control, we let wisdom make an appearance and guide us.

Unfortunately, the stress and pace of our modern lives does not often afford us the space to practise our self-control; without it, we just react with whatever comes to our heads or hearts first, and that is not necessarily the best thing. Too many of us spend our time in reaction mode: we throw tantrums, flip our middle fingers, fling harsh remarks or hateful speech at our human brothers and sisters. This just causes further stress and disunity, as one person's anger knocks against those who are in the immediate vicinity. It is therefore beholden on us now, more than ever, to hone our self-control in whatever way we can.

Every year, in the ninth month of the Islamic calendar, Muslims all over the world observe Ramadan. During this month of fasting, prayer, reflection and community, I practise my self-control. From dawn to sunset, I abstain from food, drink and sex. All the while, I do my best to control what I say, what I see, what I hear, and what I do. I try to drive ill feelings from my heart, avoid conversations filled with anger, and keep my head clear of wrongful thinking. It's a high target and, to be honest, I am far from reaching it—but every year I try. The good thing about a lofty aim is that it inspires you to keep trying. Every year I do my best to become a better person, and even if I only make small gains that is still an improvement for me and for others.

One of the ways I exercise my self-control is by meeting what is evil with that which is better. This Quranic teaching is not limited to one bad action, but applies to every bad action. It tells me that I should always respond to hate with love. It is what Allah has commanded me to do. If someone is angry towards me, I must be calm. If they want to fight me, I must retreat in peace. If someone hates me, I must love them. If someone kills my wife, I must forgive them.

THE KILLER GAVE US HIS hate, but we gave him love.

Our love grew and grew and grew, spreading far beyond our shores.

Together, New Zealanders replaced one hate with many millions of loves.

We chose love without limits, and our love triumphed.

Let us continue making the right choice. Let us choose every day what is best.

25.

Our shared duty

And We did not send you [O Prophet], except as mercy to all creatures. (Al-Quran 21:107)

And indeed We have honoured the children of Adam. (Al-Quran 17:70)

THE MESSAGE THAT WE MUST spread love, not hate, is not just mine. It is yours too. Will you take up the call? Will you spread the message of love, in your words and in your actions? Will you take the story that you have read in these pages and use it to inspire you to be loving, brave and kind, even when the worst happens? I hope you will.

The message of love and forgiveness is always necessary. It is not a message that you can repeat too often.

We all need to work hard to do what we can to break the chain of hate, to bring peace to our world. To do this, we must counter cruelty and evil whenever we cross it by responding with love. If we consistently meet hate with love, we will build a better world for everyone—and, most of all, for our children. We will lead them along the path of love so that they might follow in our footsteps. If we do not start that journey, who will? It is our job to choose love for the sake of everyone, now and into the future.

We all desire a brighter, better future for our children and grandchildren. We might have different ideas of specifically how that future might look, but underpinning all of the various visions will sit the notion of happiness. Right now, the world is a difficult place, and an unhappy one for many—it is beset by division, fear and inequality. Therefore, it is not much surprise that we see so much suffering, so much disappointment and complaint and disaccord. There is no end to a cycle like that. To find happiness for all, to bring about peace, we must interrupt that cycle with love. If we truly want to build a better future, we must love and forgive. It will not necessarily be easy, but it is necessary.

There is nothing new about hate, or about fighting and killing. There is nothing new about responding to violence with anger, or with a desire for revenge or retaliation. But just because those things are as old as humankind does not mean that they are right. Hate met with hate only sours our relationships with our human brothers and sisters. We must rise above that hate to be better, to choose what is best: love. Bitter feuds fuelled by anger and hatred only cause harm, but we can stop that harm through the power of forgiveness. Love and forgiveness can heal old wounds, and stop new ones from festering.

So, let us choose love, not hate. Let us forgive and find unity, rather than continuing to fight and further divide. This is my message, and it is yours now, too.

PERHAPS YOU ARE SAYING TO yourself, 'Forgiveness is admirable, something the Prophet (peace be upon him) could do, but I am just a simple person. My heart is not as big as the Prophet's, and I am not capable of something so admirable.'

If that's the case, let me say this: I am sorry, but you are wrong. You *do* have a big heart. It is big like mine is, big like the Prophet's (peace be upon him). You just need to use it. Please, do not underestimate yourself. You, too, are capable of great and limitless love. You, too, are capable of forgiveness.

Our world is full of so many examples of hate, and of hateful actions, but it is also filled with love. Friday 15 March 2019 saw an act of horrendous hate, a hate that took the lives of 51 innocent people and injured a nation. However, out of the ashes of that tragedy rose something incredible: love, powerful and un-conditional. Love survived the murder and destruction. It outlived the hate, and it always will. In that fact lies our hope. No act of hate will ever erase true love. Often, as was the case with 15 March, it is in response to hate that the greatest love can be born.

That day, a man who had chosen hate killed my wife. He shot her in the back while she was saving others, while she was searching for me. My wife was brave and loving, but what he did was cowardly and misguided. In the words of our imam, it broke my heart but it did not break me. It did not change me from a loving person into a cruel one. I am still kind, still loving, and that's why I forgave my wife's killer. If hope lies in love, then forgiveness is the gate we open to access that hope.

I know that people need hope. I know that there are more people in our world who are hungry for love than there are people who want the blood of their human brothers and sisters on their hands. The vast majority of us want to know how to forgive, because we don't want to be like a killer who listens only to hate. We want this no matter where we live, where we come from, what groups we fall into. The desire for love unites us.

I know this because I have seen it. It is there in the overwhelming response to my message of love and forgiveness after my wife's death. People have asked, over and over, why and how I forgave, and they ask this because they want to understand. They want hope. They just sometimes have trouble finding it.

When I chose love, and when I forgave my wife's killer, I also wanted to give our world hope. We cannot change the fact that the attack of 15 March 2019 happened, but we can act to prevent such tragedies in our future. I do not want anyone to suffer the pain that I have suffered, that my family has suffered, that every person touched by the consequences of that one man's hate has suffered. However, if our sacrifice gives birth to a better, more loving world, we will have found a way to transform hate into love.

Choose love, my brothers and sisters.

Choose love.

Tributes
to Husna

Shifa Ahmed, Husna's beloved daughter

Memories

My mother played a vital role in the development of the person I am. Although strict, she was determined to ensure that my childhood would be better than her own. She was often sick, but she always spent time with me and was always by my side whenever I needed her. She was also obsessed with my education. My mother did not have the chance to pursue higher education, despite being very intelligent. She wanted the best for me, so she would spend hours making me study and organising extra lessons for me so that I could have a comfortable life later on. She also became very overprotective, especially when it came to my friends. She would rarely allow me to hang out with my friends outside of school, saying, 'You have all that time at school to be with your friends, and that is enough, otherwise they will learn too much about you.' At the time I thought she was being extreme, but I soon realised that spending too much time with friends could make me abandon my studies and slowly fall behind.

My mother never allowed me to go anywhere unless under the eye of an adult (usually her). When she heard that high-school students have to go on camp without their parents, she went out of her way to talk to the teachers and pleaded with them to take her with us on camp. I was heavily embarrassed by this but, being the stubborn person she was, she kept on trying until eventually she had to stop. When I agreed to go on a school exchange trip to Japan, she grilled the teachers about my safety, and she would often joke, 'I am small enough, so I can easily fit in your suitcase and I can come with you.'

The main reason behind her not wanting me to go to these places without her was that she was afraid I might get hurt, or even sexually assaulted because I was a female. Because of all these constraints, I sometimes got frustrated with my mother and felt trapped, and we would often disagree about things, but I knew that she did all this because she cared so much about me.

My mother was also the sweetest person to ever exist. She had a certain charm to her that made people love her immediately, allowing her to hold any type of conversation with anyone she came across. Even if she felt sick, she would always go out of her way to help people in her community. And every day after school, ever since I started primary, she would ask how my day went. For some reason, she thoroughly enjoyed hearing about my day, and she would share my news excitedly with her friends.

My mother was a prankster, too. She loved embarrassing me, and I can still clearly remember the mischievous face she pulled after each prank, her cheeky laughter filling the room. Due to that, she was also a very good mood setter. If the aura of a room felt odd, she would crack a joke that was sure to make everyone smile. She was also very brave, and she always took action on any issues. Her confidence and wits were what gave her the inspiration, on the day of the attack, to take the risk of leading some of the women to safety, which was a phenomenal thing for her to do. There are times when I am amazed at her sheer mental strength.

I have so many other iconic memories of her, but they simply cannot be expressed on paper.

I knew she loved me very much, and I am proud to say that she was the perfect example of what a mother should be.

How did I react on the day of the attack?

During the lockdown at school, I initially thought it was just a drill, so I was rather laidback and I used the time to think about my upcoming science assessment. I got more suspicious when my biology teacher took me aside and said, 'I just got a call, and the person wanted to let you know that your father is okay.' From then on, I felt anxiety creeping up on me. *Did something bad happen?* I wondered. *Why haven't I received the same message about my mother?*

As we hid in the computer bay, shrouded in darkness with very little light to illuminate the room, I snuck underneath a table and broke the number-one rule of a lockdown, which is not to use your device. I turned on my phone and quickly toned down the brightness so no one would notice. My closest friend crawled in beside me and watched as I nervously opened Google and searched for the Christchurch news. Suddenly the feed was flooded with articles about the shooting, and I dropped my phone. I could feel tears welling in my eyes and my throat closing up as I struggled to breathe.

The first thing that came to mind was that my father must have been hurt somehow—he is a paraplegic and might not have been able to escape. I did not think of my mother at the time, because I knew that she had the ability to run and that she was the type to lead others to safety (and I was correct with that theory). People around me noticed how I was feeling, and they all reassured me that my father was fine; hence the call my teacher had received. I told myself to calm down but, even after our teachers allowed us to use the computers to entertain ourselves, I couldn't help but fidget nervously.

The car trip home was strange. I bombarded my aunt with questions about my father, and she assured me that he was in perfect health. Then I asked about my mother. My aunt kept quiet, and I decided to change the subject as I felt an awkwardness seeping into the atmosphere. I babbled about random topics, but in my head I knew something was not right.

When my aunt pulled up in the driveway, it was clear that something was very wrong. There were many cars surrounding our house and in our driveway. Our door was open, and I saw my father waiting there, as well as some other people who were leaving.

Joyous to see my father after being so concerned about his safety, I ran up the stairs and hugged him. His grim face was an indication of what was to come, because the next thing I asked was: 'Where is Mum?'

I saw my father's jaw tremble, then he broke into tears and said, 'She is with Allah.'

I could feel time stop ticking as a mix of emotions welled up inside of me. Unable to hold back, I screamed so loud that I was sure the whole neighbourhood could hear.

'Are you telling me that I no longer have a mother?' I asked. 'No, you must be lying,' I repeated, over and over again. I kept on thinking about how I was going to survive without my mother when I depended on her so much.

Realising that the physical bond between mother and daughter had been snapped, I forcefully pried open my father's arms and ran straight to my bedroom, flinging myself onto the bed, where I cried even more.

So many things were going through my head, but then I heard the faint voice of my mother calling out to me, saying not to worry. I remembered her explaining to me how I should react if she ever passed on. Recalling that memory and imagining her voice helped me to relax. I felt courage surge through me, and I took the initiative to contact my closest friends and let them know what had happened. Obviously, I cried as I told them, but I felt more at ease in my heart. The deed had already been done and nothing would bring my mother back, so why should I succumb to depression and sadness?

I remember my younger cousin running up to me, concern

plastered all over her face, so I decided to suck it up and smile. My father, through tears, told me: 'I will be your mother and father from now on.' I had to nod and accept that this was the reality, and that I would have to adapt to my new life, motherless.

The next few weeks were very difficult. I refused to talk much about my feelings or to visit a therapist. I knew that I was capable of handling my feelings by myself. I avoided meeting people, because every time they looked at me in sympathy I felt that they were expecting me to cry in front of them, and I didn't want to do that. Time passed slowly, so I talked to my closest friends and spent hours on my phone, aimlessly scrolling through videos. I also spent time praying for my mother: praying that she is granted the highest level in heaven, and that her life in her grave will be comfortable.

Unfortunately, I spent so much time thinking about how to move on that I completely disregarded my sleep cycle and my diet, and I got sick. I fell into a severe fever, which caused me to blurt out everything I had been bundling up inside.

After recovering from the fever, I swore to myself that I would look after my health, and that I would find something else to invest my time in so that I wouldn't think too deeply of my grief for my mother.

How did I move on and change my mentality to positivity?

My mother raised me in a strict yet very affectionate way, and she also put many hours into expanding my Islamic knowledge. Because my mother had Crohn's, she was constantly in and out of the hospital, and she would talk to me about the subject of death, especially after her first major surgery. We talked about what

I should do if she was ever to die suddenly. She advised me to remember that fate cannot be changed, and that I would have to think positively and pray for her next life.

Even though those conversations were uncomfortable, they really prepared me for the emotional roller-coaster I was about to go on. Knowing that my mother was killed in the most respectful and honourable way (in the eyes of Islam) helped me not to feel sad or regretful. She died a martyr (*shaheedah*) because she was fulfilling religious acts for our God, Allah, at the time of her death. In return for their acts, Allah bestows upon martyrs the greatest privileges in Paradise.

Using that information, I was able to move on from my sadness more quickly. I wanted to stay strong-willed for my mother's sake. I knew that her life from the grave to the Day of Judgement would be peaceful. She would not want me to be upset over her death, but instead happy that she did not have to suffer anymore (before she died, she had been about to have another operation). Each time I felt myself feeling sad I would think about her teaching, and it instantly made me feel more courageous.

So, now, I have moved on. Yes, there are times when I feel sad, and sometimes I cry, but that is because I miss seeing her in person and hearing her voice, not because of her death.

In terms of how I am coping now, I have changed drastically. I was a clingy child who depended heavily on my mother—she was like a pillar on which I could always lean for security and support. My mother would encourage me to be confident, but because she was always by my side I did not have the need to display any confidence; she had enough to mask any lack of confidence in me.

She would also do a lot of chores for me so that I could focus on studying. With her gone, I've had to adapt and become more independent, juggling chores, study and social activities (after the attack, I decided to follow in my mother's footsteps by being more outgoing). In truth, I have improved myself in a way that would be sure to make my mother proud if she were still here.

I still have not sought out any therapy; I stick to talking mainly to my dad about my feelings. To this day, the incident is still a bit shocking. For anyone else who has lost someone close, the best advice is to talk about your problems and to always think of the positives—otherwise, you might be dragged into a deep void full of depression and grief. Fate is fate, and we can never change what is in store for us, so we have to accept it and move on with smiles on our faces.

Dr Mustafa Farouk, President of the Federation of Islamic Associations of New Zealand (FIANZ)

I have known Sister Husna and her family for many years. I get reminded of the family at least once a week, mainly on Fridays when I receive the usual message from their email address, which is shared by Farid, Husna and their daughter, Shifa. The emails are almost always some form of reminder of our duties as Muslims to God and to our fellow human beings, or an explanation of a verse or chapter of the Quran or the sayings of our Prophet (Sallallahu Alaihi Wasallam; may the blessings and peace of Allah be upon him). These much-expected emails used to reach me on Friday afternoons or evenings and would be one of the last emails I read before turning off my computer for the day or the weekend. Sadly, and for obvious reasons, I did not receive one from that very familiar address on Friday 15 March 2019.

Although I have since resumed receiving the emails from Farid, I know Husna is not looking over his shoulder when he pushes the send button. The emails still remind me of the family, but now I think of Sister Husna more in terms of what I know of her as Farid's wife and Shifa's mum, as a community worker, and I think of Sister Husna for her selfless and courageous act on that fateful day of 15 March 2019, when she was martyred trying to help others escape the killer's weapon at al-Noor mosque in Christchurch. May God Almighty grant her the best place in Paradise. Ameen.

As a wife, Husna was the pillar of support for her husband, who became wheelchair-bound shortly after their marriage. She was what one calls 'a superwoman' and a perfect example of what a marriage partner should be. Her support in and outside their home enabled her husband to contribute to the Muslim community and New Zealand at large through his homeopathic practice, his teachings and writings, and the many other voluntary activities he is involved with. These are activities which are beyond the capacity of most individuals with no physical handicaps, but which he was able to discharge while bound to a wheelchair, with the help of his wife, Husna.

As a community person, Sister Husna worked tirelessly and was involved in many activities to do with supporting the needy, bridge-building with the wider Christchurch society and educating younger members of the Muslim community. From what I gathered from the Christchurch community, she was 'a doer not a talker', she brought boundless energy into whatever activity or project she was involved with, and she motivated those around her to always do their best. With her martyrdom, the Christchurch volunteering scene has lost one of its ground workers and champions.

Husna's heroic act on 15 March 2019 was exemplary, but not unexpected of her considering that when she was alive she always put others' interests above her own. On that day during Friday prayers when the gunman opened fire, I understand that Sister Husna managed to lead some women and children out to safety and away from the gunman; however, instead of staying put at the safe location she went back into the mosque to help Farid escape, and that was when she was martyred. As I think of Husna's sacrifice on that day and compare her to others from our Islamic history, I liken her to Naila Farafsa (may Allah be pleased with her), the fearless and articulate wife of the third rightly guided Caliph of Islam, Usman ibn Affan (may Allah be pleased with him). Naila lost her fingers protecting her husband from the swords of assassins. She held on to him tightly on her lap until he died. Following her husband's death and her recovery from injury, Naila led a group of virtuous and courageous women to the mosque and eloquently and forcefully addressed the men, demanding justice. She remained one of the most heroic women of Islam. Husna Farid Ahmed continued the legacy of protecting others heroically, as Naila did during her time. May God grant both Naila and Husna the highest places in Paradise.

My conversation with Farid Ahmed on the martyrdom of Husna when I paid him a condolence visit will remain in my memory forever. After he reminded us of two of the relevant verses of the

Quran fit for the occasion, he added: 'Husna has been a wonderful wife to me, and I have always prayed for her to have the best place in Paradise; with her martyrdom, I am happy my prayers will be fulfilled, God willing.'

In Islam we remember our heroes, martyrs and loved ones through prayers. May Husna's memory and the memory of all those who lost their lives at the Christchurch shootings live on, and may Allah grant them the highest place in Jannah-paradise. And may Allah grant their families the repose to bear their loss.

Dave Woodbury, Christchurch Police

It is truly a privilege to be asked by Farid to contribute to this book acknowledging Husna's life. It is also challenging, as I'm not sure that I can appropriately verbalise what an incredible human being Husna was, and always will be.

I first met Farid and Husna about a decade ago, when I was the community constable for the Addington/Hillmorton area. I cannot remember the precise circumstances of how we first became acquainted, but I somehow ended up having refreshments inside their house, and feeling incredibly welcomed. From that day onward, I became friends with their family, and developed a tremendous respect for the contribution they made to the community.

The latter part of my police career saw me move from community policing to the field of domestic violence. Needless to say, this new field had many challenges. A particularly challenging part of this field is understanding how to tackle domestic violence among different ethnicities. Both Farid and Husna were tremendously helpful to me with some very difficult cases I had involving the Muslim community. They were equally welcoming to my family-violence colleagues, Julie Crequer, Kevin Holder and Juliette Hunter. These colleagues adored this family. Husna and Farid gave their time willingly, and my colleagues and I are eternally grateful to them for this.

If I fast-forward to the day of the terrible tragedy at the mosques, one of my most immediate thoughts was for Husna, Farid, Farhana and Shifa. I was perhaps most concerned for Farid's well-being, as I thought being wheelchair-bound would have made it difficult for him to escape. I sent him an email within an hour of the tragedy, simply saying how sorry and heartbroken I was, and that I hoped he was OK. I did not hear back from him for some days, as naturally he had other pressing priorities. In the meantime, I was taken into a private room by my colleague Kevin Holder, and advised that Farid was alive, as were Farhana and Shifa. My relief was short-lived, as Kevin advised me that Husna was one of the victims who had been killed. It is very difficult to describe how I felt, but I recall immediately saying, 'The world has lost an angel.' I think those six words are incredibly accurate when describing Husna. An angel to me is somebody of exemplary conduct and virtue, a guiding spirit, and a person who leaves an indelible mark on the world. Husna is all of those things, and many more. I openly admit to shedding tears when reading about the heroic nature of Husna on the day of the tragedy. She died as she lived, always thinking of others, and putting others before herself. The world was a better place for having Husna in it, and I am a better person for having known Husna. Indeed: the world has lost an angel.

Nasrin and Yusuf Joarder, friends

Looking back, from the very first day she set foot on New Zealand soil to now, we've known Husna Ahmed for roughly 25 years. Living in a foreign country far from home would've brought much difficulty, but *Mashallah* [as God has willed it] she grew in both skills and wisdom over the years. She went on to become the 'Mother Teresa' of the Muslim community in Christchurch. Her motto was to prioritise others before herself. There is no doubt she has gone straight to Jannah. We are proud of her.

Ayesha Corner, Husna's sister-in-law

Someone said to me that Husna was a philanthropist—not just a volunteer, not just someone who helped the community, she was more than that—so I wanted to delve more into what a philanthropist is. When I looked at the definition of a philanthropist it helped me to understand.

The definition of a philanthropist is 'a person who seeks to promote the welfare of others'. It means generosity in all its forms, and is often defined as giving gifts of time, talent and treasure to help make life better for other people.

Wow, this definition really drives home how much of a philanthropist Husna truly was. Husna may not have had a lot of money but she devoted all her time to helping others in so many different ways.

Where do I start? What was so special about Husna? Why does everyone remember her so fondly? What did she do? Why do people call her a heroine?

I first met Husna back at the beginning of 1999. I was brought to meet her and her husband, Farid, at their place, and the first thing about her was her brilliant smile and her hospitality. I was fed with beautiful food that she had cooked, and given wonderful company by them both. At the time I was not a Muslim and I was struggling with my own personal issues and faith. Husna listened, and from then she worked to help me feel that I belonged, and I regularly visited them to learn about Islam until I converted in March 1999.

I went through some struggles, and they invited me to stay with them for three months, helping me through all these struggles until I was able to manage on my own again. Husna taught me how to make chapati and several different ways to make curry. She looked after me and helped me to get strong again.

About a year later Husna introduced me to her brother, and he and I subsequently got married, so she was always there for me, supporting me in any way I needed. I was honoured to be a part of their family.

Over the years, I have been astounded with the service of Husna. Her whole life revolved around supporting and helping others, as well as caring for her husband after his terrible accident left him paralysed in 1998. She always had a smile, nothing was ever too hard, and she was a leader. She never got paid to do all the work in the community; she did this with love and gave up her time to help anyone who crossed her path.

Mother—I would best describe Husna as a mother to the community. Even though she was just 20 when she arrived in New Zealand, she was a carer to all people. She loved everyone. She had only been in New Zealand for four years when her husband had his accident and they had to move to Christchurch. I met her not long after that, and she was already someone to look up to. As time went by, people would visit her, ask for her help, and she would feed people, care for people, advise people and listen to people. She was strong.

She was also blessed by Allah with a daughter in 2004. She was a great mother: stern but gentle, loving and kind. She raised her daughter to be a great young lady who is also strong, sensible, intelligent and has inherited her mother's wonderful smile. Her daughter never missed out on mothering even though Husna spent so much time helping others. This just goes to show how special Husna was.

Sickness—Husna suffered her own ill health with Crohn's disease and had to have an operation in her last year with us, but her sickness never stopped her. I remember telling her to slow down, but she just couldn't say no and would never let someone else suffer if she could help them in any way possible.

Translator—Husna spent a lot of time with women in the Bangladeshi community: going with them to their doctors, helping with their pregnancies, going shopping, and attending births so she could translate for the mothers-to-be. She was there for many births and saw a lot of Bangladeshi children come into this world. She continued to help these mothers whenever they called. Whether it was the early hours of the morning or late at night, Husna always went out of her way to be there for them.

Organiser—Husna organised many events for Eid, Aqiqah (childbirth ceremonies), and for the Bangla community here in

Christchurch. She would help to organise the children to perform these events; it was her speciality. She had so much patience with the children, and you could see the joy in her eyes when helping them perform. Her smile and enjoyment were infectious, and I loved watching her with the children. She was always busy at these events: helping set them up, organising the structure of the events, organising the preparation and delivery of food to everyone, and organising everyone when cleaning up the premises.

Teacher—Husna taught children every week over the past 20 years. She would teach them their letters and small chapters from the Quran. She gave up many hours to help children learn the basics of Islam. She would teach them the steps of prayer, what to say, what to do, and what the meaning and importance of prayer was. I remember her doing this: she was stern but also caring, and children were attracted to her like a magnet. They loved her, and she would take them under her arm and guide them. It was clear that children always felt safe with her.

She would also organise meetings with women to teach them how to perform the wrapping of a sister who has died. She would take us through the steps of the process. Sometimes she would show us with a doll, and then she would have some fun and get one of us to lie on the cloth so she could show us how to wash and wrap a body. She also showed us how to cut the cloth so we could have it ready for after the washing.

Because of her teachings I was able to perform the final act of helping to wash and wrap her body for burial. I had seen her do it several times in her teaching sessions, and to do this for her was a great honour, to be able to repay her with the respect she so deserved, to thank her for all her service, her help, her support and the love she gave me.

Sacrifice—Husna sacrificed so much. Her whole life, she sacrificed for others. She sacrificed her time, her health, and in her final piece of work on this earth she sacrificed her life for her husband.

On 15 March 2019 when 51 people died in the al-Noor and Linwood mosques, she was one of those who returned to Allah on that day. She worked on getting women and children out of the mosque while all the shooting was happening. But that was not enough! She went back into the mosque to find her husband, she wanted to make sure he was safe. That third time going back she sacrificed her life trying to find him. Allah gave her the highest honour and took her while she was helping others.

Our dear Husna, she was the best of us. She donated all her time, her health, her support, her love to all of humankind. Anyone who met her loved her, and was astounded with her hospitality, generosity, and her love for others. She treated people with kindness, and always had a great big genuine smile.

The translation of Husna means 'the best' and she was indeed the best of us. She was someone who the young and the old could look up to, and we would all aim to be like her. It was an honour and privilege to know Husna and be a part of her family.

Shawna Stewart, former student at Shifa's school

[To Husna:] Hearing about the news of your passing was devastating. I sincerely thank you for looking after me and all the other students while on camp in year 5 and 6. I remember you would make sure we all ate our dinner, and that we had sunscreen on before we went out to play. I remember coming to your house once and playing with your daughter. I remember you made us samosas, and they were delicious! Thank you for being so kind, caring and loving to everyone around you. YOU ARE US. May you rest in peace.

Lina, Kim and family, community members

We need more people like Husna in this world. She is a HERO in New Zealand hearts.

Lesley Sales, homeopath

In 1998 Husna was dealing with a very difficult situation: Farid was in intensive care at Christchurch Hospital, having been struck by a car while crossing the road in the early hours of the morning. The car had been doing 99 kilometres per hour and Farid had extensive injuries—he was not expected to live. Husna was looking for a homeopath to give assistance, and a friend referred her to me.

I met Husna at the hospital and we went into the intensive care ward to see Farid. In addition to concussion, chest injuries, both legs broken and extensive contusions, his back was broken. The medical staff had outlined the extent of the damage: he was deeply sedated, in an induced coma, and had been assessed as having a seven per cent chance of survival.

Husna and I retired to the waiting room. I told her that we could probably fix everything quite quickly except the spinal break.

'If that is the case,' I said, 'he will likely spend the rest of his life in a wheelchair and, if he does, you will be the one who will have to cope with that. Is that what you want?'

Without a moment's hesitation: 'Yes,' she said. She faced an uncertain future with rare courage and utter selflessness. Carefully, tenderly, she sat by Farid's bed and administered faithfully the remedies that I brought, and we watched him recover over the next ten days. At that point the medical staff considered him ready to go on to the spinal unit at Burwood.

Husna showed application and devotion to Farid, and determination to go the extra mile for those she set out to help. She had a strong sense of values and was prepared to stand up for them in the face of opposition. She extended compassion and care towards those in need, and she faced the world with integrity and grace. No one who came to her for help, in genuine need, would be sent away empty-handed.

At times she seemed radiant: a quiet joy emanated from her being and shone out on those around her. This was not a passive state—she believed in taking action, dealing with issues as they arose, helping others, solving problems, and she could be quite firm and definite about the right course of action to be taken. With a quiet courage she faced any difficulties that confronted her, with no sign of self-pity or a desire to avoid problems. At no point did she ever put herself ahead of others or show signs of selfishness. She had a smile and a kind word for everyone.

When the gunman came, it is significant that Husna was not trying to run away to save herself—she was killed while looking to save Farid.

The world has lost a very bright soul and is the poorer for it. But there will be a new star in the sky: Husna has walked back into the arms of God.

Marama, Meshary and Mughren, former students in Husna's class

On memories of Aunty Husna: If an angel existed physically on earth, Aunty Husna's presence, her kindness, her gentleness contributed to this being her. Her humble way of being was approachable, her kind checking-in with how you are doing was beautiful. She had this amazing, loving and caring nature that you felt from her and it was touching. Aunty Husna, you will be always remembered as a lovely influence in our lives. As will your family and the beautiful experiences we had with you all.

Sarah Saad Al-Harran, Muslim community member

May Allah (the glorious most high) grant Aunty Husna a high status in Jannah—she was indeed a good role model and inspiration to all us younger women.

Jill Wilby, homeopath

I am a colleague of Farid Ahmed, and through him have known Husna for thirteen years. Farid and Husna hosted our monthly peer-group meetings during that time. Our last meeting was a week before Husna's death and none of us ever entertained the idea that it would be the last time we saw her. I still see her popping her head around the door to tell Farid she was off on the school run.

When I think of Husna I am reminded of her kindness, warmth, thoughtfulness, intelligence and compassion. I see her cheeky smile and hear her infectious laugh. She was a most caring, considerate woman, but also had a fun side to her. As a support to Farid in his faith, his health and their community she was exemplary. As a mother she was fiercely proud and protective. Not only did she mother her own child but also others in the Muslim community.

Sudden death is always a shock, but sudden, violent death is abhorred. To think this kind, gentle, beautiful woman died in such a cruel fashion is beyond words. The only goodness that can come from this event is for all people to come together to promote love, respect, generosity, tolerance and kindness. We can all do it.

When I think of Husna now I see a white dove, and I know that this is the most fitting symbol for who she was and what she represented. Husna, thank you for your friendship and love. Rest in peace and arohanui.

Kathy Dwyer, physiotherapist

I was incredibly sad to hear about Husna's death. She was such a lovely, caring and strong woman. She will be hugely missed.

Trish Clarke, property manager

Husna was a very lovely lady.

Yasmin Begum and Tuhedul Islam,
Bangladeshi study circle members

Dear Sister Husna, we did not have any blood relationship with you, but we had a *heart* relationship with you. You established our study circle to tie everyone's hearts together with the thread of love and good actions. It was your dream circle. Our circle was nourished with your selfless love and guidance.

You are not dead in our hearts; you never will be. You will be alive always in our memory. Your loving actions will be alive with us forever. We shall carry on your dream circle for continuing good actions, *Insha Allah.*

Gulshan Huk, former women's co-ordinator at
Muslim Association Canterbury

The first time I met Sister Husna was in the mosque, where every Jumu'ah day she helps all the ladies and organises for Jumu'ah. From that first day in the mosque, she helped me and gave me good advice, and my son Ilfaaz started attending the Quran classes held by Brother Farid and Sister Husna. Over the past 20 years, we became so close and started sharing our personal matters. And she was my mentor. Losing her is a very big loss to our community. Because of her, I served the mosque for three years as women's co-ordinator, and we formed a women's Janazah team which we all want to continue. In every step she was willing to help. To describe her is too difficult as she was a very intelligent, helpful person, and to find someone like her is very hard. She will always be in my heart, and will never, ever be forgotten. And she is not only in my heart but everyone she has met would be missing her. Allah may give my sister the highest ranking in Jannah. All our *du'a* and blessings upon her, as she has left a good work behind which we shall continue.

Rhonda Hamilton-Cross, homeopath

Husna was such a kind, loving soul whose natural beauty and charm filled the room. She was an awesome cook who loved to provide.

I was very fortunate to have known her. The following acrostic poem has words which truly reflect in my mind who she was. Happy memories will always remain.

Honest, heartfelt, hard-working, helpful
Understanding, uplifting, unselfish, universal
Sympathetic, sincere, special, supportive.
Nurturing, natural, non-violent, nourishing
Affable, amiable, accommodating, adaptable

Muhammad Hafijur Rahman, parent of students in Husna's class

How was Sister Husna to us? She was always smiley and kind. We used to consider her our guardian. We called her whenever we were in trouble, and she always ran to us with comfort and solutions.

We will not forget the way she helped my wife during her pregnancy, right up to the delivery. Furthermore, her visits to cut the hair of our newborn baby and her generous advice on how to take care of our baby.

Here we live in a foreign country. But Husna's presence made us feel that she was our caring family guardian. We never thought we would find someone like her, who would care for us as if we were family members.

Every Sunday, we used to take our children to Husna in the mosque class. Our children would run towards her for a hug. She was fond of our children, as they were of her. She taught our children free of charge, and we are so grateful for that.

She also used to take my daughter Hafsa to her home. Hafsa learned many things from Husna, and we were very happy having her around. But alas! Her loss devastated my children, my wife and me.

We shall never find a replacement for Husna. We are saddened. We pray to Allah to grant her Paradise. Ameen!

Felicia, neighbour

I feel very honoured to have spent the last year or so sharing the same space with and getting to know Farid and Husna, and to have witnessed the peaceful grace and unwavering assistance Husna showed everyone so selflessly.

They say people enter our lives for a reason, a season or a lifetime. Very few could be classed as all three—and yet Husna is one of those rare friends. A person who touched lives in such a way that your day was all the brighter from simply a smile and a wave through the kitchen window.

Husna and her family came into my life when I needed my own sanctuary, a place I could just 'be'. I was welcomed with warmth and generosity, and allowed to go about my life quietly while knowing that if I needed anything I just had to ask. Briefly I called them my landlords; very soon I thought of them as friends.

Through our chats under the washing line or in the garden, I learned of Husna's life, her work, her family, her spirit, and her ability to connect with people from all stages and all walks of life. She was generous to a fault, giving her everything to helping the community around her—many times her own health or needs taking a back seat.

Husna, you will always be a special presence in my life. I shall keep your memory burning alive in my heart, and your beautiful spirit will remind me of the joy in helping your neighbour and making them a friend.

Indra, friend

I have known Husna briefly and in that short period of time she made an impact on me as a person who was very selfless, caring and compassionate. Her outlook on life was very positive and meaningful. To serve the community at large was always foremost in her life.

Her death came as a shock but I knew she died for a good cause. I will remember her as the smiling personality—a loving and caring friend.

Natasha Mitchell, former journalism student

In 2003 I was studying journalism at Canterbury University and I interviewed Farid Ahmed, along with several other members of the Christchurch Muslim community, for an article later published in the *Christchurch Mail*. I remember meeting Farid at the mosque at the end of Sunday lessons, then visiting his family home. Husna had cooked curried lamb, and she kindly made a mild version for me while they had a spicier version. Over the meal, we talked. Husna didn't say much, but I remember her kindness, her warmth and humility, and how happy she was that I enjoyed the meal. Husna was pregnant when we met and I knew she would become a loving mother.

[To Farid:] I was, and still am all these years later, so grateful to you both for opening your home and your hearts to me for that story.

Rabeya Begum, parent of student in Husna's class

Husna Apa [Sister] was my daughter's Arabic teacher, and she taught my daughter and also other children free of cost, which was unexpected to me. I remember that the Prophet Muhammad (may the blessings and peace of Allah be upon him) said, 'The best of you are those who learn the Quran and teach it.'

On the afternoon of 14 March [the day before she was killed] I met with her in my friend's house. That day she brought some food for us.

She was an iron lady. She helped everyone in any matter. I could not forget her. I am speechless and literally heartbroken by hearing the news of Husna Apa passing away. May Allah reward her for all her good deeds and grant her the highest of ranks in Jannah.

Tina Rachael, neighbour

Husna was an amazing, loving, giving lady, so gracious. She gave me endless help with my grandson Cayleb at Spreydon School, and I shall dearly miss her smiles, waves and talks at Riccarton.

Donna Roy, massage therapist

I wish to express my condolences for the loss of Husna, a wonderful wife and mother.

Hisham Musa, Muslim community member

Our sister Husna died a martyr, trying to save lives. All the years we have known her she's been a person who cares. Her house stayed open for anyone who needed any help at any time: anyone hungry, cold, sick; a woman who just delivered a baby; a family who needed any help; they were all welcome even when she didn't know them. And yes, she would've forgiven her killer for sure. That I know.

Our sister Husna has been martyred in the Masjid al-Noor attack. Her house has been open to the needy and the hungry, and she has sustained orphans and assisted her husband. They both taught the Muslim kids in the mosque for more than 20 years. She was very humble and one of the purest of hearts here in Christchurch. Always smiling and never mentioning anyone except in good ways. Pray for her and her husband and daughter.

Diane, homeopath

Husna was a bright and beautiful friend. Over the years, I had many delicious lunches prepared with love by her at our meetings held in their family home. She always greeted me with 'How are you?' and was always keen to hear what was happening in my life. She genuinely cared for others—this was clearly demonstrated on the day of her passing.

She has touched many people's lives and is remembered fondly for her warmth and charisma, and will never be forgotten. I hold treasured memories of Husna. It was a fourteen-year friendship with many shared life experiences.

Sally Keen, ACC receptionist

I will always remember Husna coming in. Husna always had a smile on her face and was so cheery. It was a pleasure to chat with her on those occasions.

Dr Chalmers-Watson, Nurse Kirsten and the Gastro team

We remember Husna as brave and determined in the face of her Crohn's disease.

Tiresa Sio, student in Husna's class

May Allah (the glorious most high) shine the brightest light in dear Husna's grave and grant her the highest rank in Jannat al-Firdaus [the top layer of Paradise]. Farid and Husna's love story will be one of the most treasured stories to tell, as one cannot talk about one without the other.

Beloved Sister Husna and her husband, Farid, were my Quran teachers who became a great source of support to me in my journey as a revert and as a friend. The beauty of these two is their patience and love for all humankind. Their strength was without any boundaries.

Farid, I can't thank you and Husna enough for being my teachers. What I shall always treasure was that Husna gave me my first prayer mat that I silently wept on, performing Salah . . . Her presence was selfless, patient, overtly generous and kind. Never, ever losing the opportunity to give to others in the community. Her smile that was so endearing and warm lifted our hearts and spirits—imprinted deep in our hearts.

Julie Gardiner, friend

Husna was a shining star who will shine brightly forever. She was always smiling. She was funny, kind, compassionate, loving and helpful. She was there for me when my late husband was very ill; she was always bringing him medicine and food for me.

Even though she was sick herself she got out of bed and went to help others. She put her grief aside and came to visit me in hospital a day after she buried her brother. That's the person she was—always there for others. She lost her life running to save her husband, not thinking of herself. She lived life to the fullest, and she achieved so much in her short life.

Forever loved, Husna, you will always be in my heart and prayers.

Chris McCausland, occupational therapist

I am so sad to hear of Husna's passing. Husna and Farid have always welcomed me into their home and I will miss seeing Husna. She was like a ray of sunshine—she had the most beautiful smile and laugh. Husna was also a very devoted wife and mother and cared deeply for her family. She always had others' best interests at heart. The world is a better place for her having been in it.

Judith Collett, gastroenterologist

I had the honour of helping Husna for several years with her Crohn's disease. I remember her bringing her beautiful baby daughter into the clinic, and her radiant smile. She also brought me homemade dishes as a thank you, which I was very touched by.

Someone once wrote: 'Empathy is your pain in my heart.' The world has lost a beautiful person, wife and mother. Please know that I am just one of many who was touched by the stardust that was Husna.

'Our way is not soft grass, it's a mountain path with lots of rocks. But it goes upwards, forward, toward the sun.' (Ruth Westheimer)

Len McGrane, friend

Husna was cheerful, intelligent, happy, hospitable and determined to be an exemplary Muslim, mother and friend.

This was obvious the very first time I met her and Farid. They had generously arranged for me and a few friends to visit Masjid al-Noor and see through the building. They demonstrated prayer, answered our questions and shared simple refreshments. Husna was welcoming and informative, relaxed and confident.

From that time on, Farid and I would sometimes meet in his home, and there Husna was the perfect hostess. Her greeting was happy, warm, sincere and dignified. Needless to say, her morning teas and lunches were refined and gracious! Husna had a way of coming into the room and greeting Farid's guests with a lightness and happiness that visitors did not forget.

The Holy Quran says, 'For those who believe and do righteous deeds, for them is happiness and a beautiful return.' (13:29) Husna's belief and righteous acts overflowed in a happiness that brought beautiful goodness to the people she met.

Melanie Lous, osteopath

[To Farid:] Husna was a beautiful soul and I feel lucky to have met the both of you.

Greg Canton, friend

I met Farid and Husna around 2008. What struck me first was what a loving, supportive family they were. Husna was an incredible wife, mother and friend, and I am sure that would have extended to anyone within her family and community. She was a very caring, strong and selfless person who always put others first. After the Christchurch earthquakes [in 2010 and 2011] Husna and Farid reached out to my family, as I am sure they would have to many others.

Husna had more of an impact on my life than she probably would have realised.

Fiona, Monet, Peter and Dennis, neighbours

[To Farid:] Your beautiful wife, Husna, was always so kind, greeting us with warm smiles when we walked by and bringing gifts to Uncle. She will be dearly missed and fondly remembered.

Madina and the Miyakhel family, former students in Husna's class

'Aunty': that's what we got taught to call you from a young age. It might have been the way you smiled, the gentle kindness in your heart or the warmth of your words that helped us associate the word 'aunty' with you.

For almost five years you would take Nagina and me to Quran classes. Within those years we learned valuable lessons about the importance of Islam. I especially loved Uncle Farid's Islamic stories. You never truly know the value of life until it has become a memory, and those good times have become a positive memory that we hold on to and cherish.

It feels weird having to write about you, Aunty, because we cannot put into words the value of your beautiful soul. You have been a mother figure for my sister and me. We will never forget your love for jalebis [Indian sweets], your love for teaching and most importantly your love for humanity! May Allah grant you the highest Paradise and give us the opportunity to meet you there.

Donna McAleer, community worker

My friend and fellow community worker, Husna Ahmed, was a frequent visitor to the Rowley Resource Centre, the community centre where I worked in Hoon Hay [in Christchurch]. We met for the first time in 2015. It was clear to me then that Husna had integrity, compassion, kindness and commitment to the community in which she lived. What was remarkable was that, as time moved on, it became obvious that her work was for altruistic reasons. It was all voluntary. Each time Husna would arrive she would be abuzz with ideas, and she always had an understanding of what was happening in the community. We developed a friendship.

What remains with me is her genuine compassion and her laughter, particularly when sharing stories of motherhood. We had a shared passion for ensuring that we work to educate and support 'our children' so that they grow and develop to be respectable citizens of the world. I know that even in her final moments, no doubt filled with fear, she shepherded women and children from the mosque and then returned to ensure her husband was safe—a decision that resulted in her death. That act alone affirms the person who she was.

Husna and I rarely shared discussions on the Quran, cultural differences or her role as a Muslim woman living her life in New Zealand. Our companionship transcended all of this—it was woman to woman. A mutual respect established.

So it was that in 2018 we cultivated an opportunity for the local Muslim women to come to our community centre to learn to speak English. Many of these women live here with their husbands, who have working visas. These women did not qualify for Ministry of Social Development-funded English language classes in the city, but they wanted to effectively integrate into our community, so we created this opportunity. Husna's focus was on empowering and ensuring that these women grew both personally and in their community engagement, beyond their connections with their Bangladeshi friends and families. Another vision of positive integration that Husna considered.

So now Husna has gone. She leaves a legacy of community connectedness, cultural awareness, respect, and a drive for Muslims to continue to grow in their faith and to become part of the Kiwi culture. This is laid out for those who she has impacted, helped, supported, taught—I am one of those disciples.

About the author

FARID AHMED has lived in New Zealand for more than 30 years. In 1998 he was run over in the street by a drunk driver. Miraculously, Farid survived, but he became a paraplegic. Despite being confined to a wheelchair, Farid is a senior leader at Masjid al-Noor, the mosque on Deans Avenue in Christchurch, and he works as a homeopath. Since the mosque attack of 15 March 2019 he has become a sought-after speaker at events around the world, where he preaches his message of forgiveness and love.

First published in 2020

Text © Farid Ahmed, 2020

Allen & Unwin
Level 2, 10 College Hill, Freemans Bay
Auckland 1011, New Zealand
Phone: (64 9) 377 3800
Email: auckland@allenandunwin.com
Web: www.allenandunwin.co.nz

83 Alexander Street
Crows Nest NSW 2065, Australia
Phone: (61 2) 8425 0100

A catalogue record for this book is available from
the National Library of New Zealand.

ISBN 978 1 98854 748 0

All photographs are from Farid Ahmed's private collection
Floral illustration on cover by Anna Paff/Shutterstock.com

Design by Kate Barraclough
Set in Adobe Caslon Pro
Printed and bound in Australia by Griffin Press, part of Ovato

1 3 5 7 9 10 8 6 4 2

MIX
Paper from
responsible sources
FSC
www.fsc.org
FSC® C009448

The paper in this book is FSC® certified.
FSC® promotes environmentally responsible,
socially beneficial and economically viable
management of the world's forests.